Augustus Mongredien

History of the Free-Trade Movement in England

Augustus Mongredien

History of the Free-Trade Movement in England

ISBN/EAN: 9783744725958

Printed in Europe, USA, Canada, Australia, Japan

Cover: Foto ©ninafisch / pixelio.de

More available books at **www.hansebooks.com**

HISTORY

OF THE

FREE-TRADE MOVEMENT

IN ENGLAND

BY

AUGUSTUS MONGREDIEN

Author of " Free Trade and English Commerce," &c.

NEW YORK

G. P. PUTNAM'S SONS

27 AND 29 WEST 23D STREET

1881

PREFACE.

ENGLAND stands in a peculiar position with respect to the Free-trade System. Its theoretical soundness and practical advantages had been proclaimed by scientific adepts for nearly a century before it was adopted and brought into actual use by the government of any country; and then, it was only by the government of one country. That country was England. In all other states, the amateurs of the science of Political Economy have set at naught the conclusions of its professors, and the action of statesmen with regard to Free Trade has been the very reverse of that advocated by the best thinkers and writers on the subject. Scientific men still persistently advocate the principle; while statesmen (save in the case of England) persistently act in opposition to it. How came England to form that exception? This, we think, should afford an interesting subject for inquiry.

It was in 1752 that David Hume laid the foundation of the science of Political Economy by the publication of his luminous essays on "Commerce," "Money," "Balance of Trade," "Taxes," &c. His treatment of those topics and of others incidentally discussed, such as "Free Trade," "Paper Money," &c., was at once logical and lucid, and exhibited his complete mastery over all these subjects. The conclusions at which he arrived respecting them were, indeed, in almost perfect accordance with those of the most advanced Economists of the present day. Twenty-four years afterwards, Adam Smith followed with his great work on the "Wealth of Nations," which appeared in 1776. Almost simultaneously, much of the same ground was broken in France by Quesnay and Turgot, whose novel views as to the freedom of commercial intercourse attracted much attention. From that period to the present time, hundreds of eminent men have made the science of Political Economy their special study, and all have concurred in denouncing the injurious effects of the protective system on the wealth of nations.

But, so far, England is the only country in which the voice of science has been listened to with any practical result. There is, indeed, in many other countries a large and increasing band of thinkers who know the truth, propagate the truth, and work for the truth; but they are, for the present, over-ridden by the indifferent many and the interested few. The physicians in vain prescribe a salutary regimen, if their patients deride their authority and ignore their injunctions. England is as yet the only patient that has conformed to the physicians' precepts, and we propose in the following pages to inquire into the results of that exceptional course of action.

This little work may also subserve another purpose. There is no allegation that is more frequently or more exultingly urged as an argument by the foreign opponents of free trade than that England has been ruined by it. True, that it is a mere allegation, unsupported by the slightest evidence; true, that statements are not facts, but, indeed, often the reverse of facts. But that does not stand in the way of our objectors. Mendacious statements, if, and as long as, they obtain credence, being, like all errors, unlimited in their range and unrestricted as to their direction, afford a wide field for declamation. Falsely assuming that, since the adoption of free trade, England has been gradually declining—that the condition of her people has greatly deteriorated—that her commerce is fast diminishing—that her wealth is melting away—and that a nation, once so flourishing, is on the eve of a total collapse, they triumphantly exclaim, "How dare you recommend to other countries that nostrum that has brought you so low? Having yourselves been ruined by free trade, you seek to inflict the same ruin on us, in order to reduce us to the same abject state. But we will enlighten our own people as to the wretched plight to which the abandonment of protection has brought you, and your case shall be to them a warning and not an example."

The best reply to this style of argument, founded, as it is, on misrepresentation, is quietly to set forth the exact truth, as embodied in historical and statistical facts of undeniable authenticity; and this we have endeavoured to do in the little volume which we now venture to present to the public.

A. MONGREDIEN.

Forest Hill, January, 1881.

CONTENTS.

CHAPTER I.
(1824 to 1826.)

Our Commercial System in 1824—Native Industry completely Protected from Foreign Competition—Import Duties on every Foreign Article—Corn Laws of 1815 and 1822—Navigation Laws—Condition of the People—Severe Commercial Crisis of 1825-1826 1

CHAPTER II.
(1827 to 1839.)

New Corn Law of 1828 merely a slight Shift in the Sliding Scale—Catholic Emancipation in 1829—Reform Bill in 1832—Lord Melbourne's Administration—Financial Crisis of 1837—Accession of Queen Victoria—Manchester Anti-Corn-Law Association formed in 1838—Mr. Villiers' Motions on the Corn Laws in February and March, 1839—Sir R. Peel's unsuccessful Attempt to Form a Ministry . 13

CHAPTER III.
(1840 to 1841.)

The Anti-Corn-Law Associations take Measures to "instruct the Nation"—Joseph Hume's Committee of Inquiry—Queen's Marriage—Labours of the Anti-Corn-Law League 23

CHAPTER IV.
(1841.)

The Whig Ministry propose a Fixed Duty of 8s. per quarter on Wheat, in lieu of the Sliding Scale—Their Budget—They are Defeated on the Sugar Duties—Dissolution of Parliament—New House of Commons—Richard Cobden—Sir Robert Peel's Administration—State of the Country—Operations of the Anti-Corn-Law League 41

CHAPTER V.
(1842.)

Sir Robert Peel's Modification of the Corn Law pleases no one—Mr. Villiers' Amendment for Entire Repeal Rejected—A Bold Budget—Income Tax imposed—Reduction of Import Duties on 750 Foreign Articles 57

CHAPTER VI.
(1842.)

First Instalment of Tariff Reform—Chartism—Its Leaders advise a general "Strike"—Its Collapse—The Anti-Corn-Law League raises £50,000 63

CHAPTER VII.
(1843.)

State of the Country—Scene between Sir R. Peel and Mr. Cobden—Activity of the Anti-Corn-Law League—Debate on Mr. Villiers' Annual Motion. 79

CHAPTER VIII.
(1843.)

The City of Durham sends Mr. John Bright to Parliament—Proceedings of the Anti-Corn-Law League, which proposes to raise £100,000 94

CHAPTER IX.
(1844.)

Meetings of the Anti-Corn-Law League—The Budget Exhibits a Surplus—Fresh Import-duty Reductions—Ministers Outvoted on the Sugar Question—Sir Robert Peel induces the House to Rescind the Vote—The League at Work on the Voting Registers 104

CHAPTER X.
(1845.)

State of Parties at the Opening of Parliament—Large Reductions in the Import Duties—Dissatisfaction of the Protectionist Party—Mr. Disraeli's Philippics—Anti-Corn-Law League Bazaar at Covent Garden Theatre—Mr. Villiers' Annual Motion 115

CHAPTER XI.
(1845.)

The League's £100,000 Fund raised—Bad Weather in September injures the English Harvest—First Appearance in Ireland of the Potato Disease—Perplexity and Indecision of Ministers—Dissensions in the Cabinet—Sir Robert Peel Resigns—Lord John Russell unable to form a Ministry—Return to Power of Sir Robert Peel—Remarks on his Position — The League proposes to raise a Fund of £250,000 132

CHAPTER XII.
(1846.)

Sir Robert Peel's bold and comprehensive Financial Measures—The remaining Import Duties again largely reduced—Total Repeal of the Corn Laws to take place in 1849, with, meanwhile, only a moderate Import Duty—Interesting Debates—Ministerial Triumph—Irish Coercion Bill—Ministerial Defeat—Resignation of Sir Robert Peel. 150

CHAPTER XIII.
(*From* 1846 *onwards.*)

Lord John Russell's Administration—Dissolution of the Anti-Corn-Law League—Measures to relieve Irish Distress—Repeal of the Navigation Laws—Gradual Abolition of remaining Protective Duties — Final Achievement of a thorough Free Trade Tariff 162

CHAPTER XIV.

Effects of Free Trade on the Prosperity of the Country—Comparative condition of England in 1840 under Protection, and in 1878 under Free Trade—Concluding Remarks . 175

HISTORY

OF THE

Free-Trade Movement in England.

CHAPTER I.

(1824 to 1826.)

Our Commercial System in 1824—Native Industry completely Protected from Foreign Competition—Import Duties on every Foreign Article—Corn Laws of 1815 and 1822—Navigation Laws—Condition of the People—Severe Commercial Crisis of 1825-1826.

DURING the quarter of a century that elapsed between the years 1824 and 1849 a most remarkable revolution took place in the commercial policy of England.

Up to the year 1824 our system had been strictly protective. We had all but prohibited the admission of foreign articles of food; we had, by excessive import duties, discouraged and curtailed the importation of all other foreign commodities; and we had practically, by our Navigation Laws, restricted our foreign trade to the use of British ships. By the close of the year 1849 we had adopted a diametrically opposite policy. We had admitted foreign grain free of all duty, except a small nominal one for registration purposes; we had abolished import duties on nearly every foreign

1824. article; and we had repealed those old Navigation Laws on which our maritime prosperity had so long been supposed to depend.

Truly a stupendous change, either for good or for evil! Its authors must indeed have been sustained by the deepest and most earnest conviction of its soundness, for they were assuming a momentous responsibility. So absolute and so sudden a reversal of the policy by which the commercial destinies of an empire had till then been guided was unprecedented. The new policy thus boldly inaugurated was untried. It was utterly condemned, strenuously opposed, and its failure confidently predicted by a numerous body of influential men. It had its foundation, not in experience, for it was an innovation: not in example, for no other country had tried it: but in the theories of thinking men, who elaborated the system in their closets. Their teachings pointed out the injurious effects of the prevailing restrictive policy, and the benefits that might be expected to flow from a policy of commercial freedom.

To British statesmen belongs the glory of having thus first applied the deductions of science to the art of government. But in so doing they had to take on themselves the risk of failure, and confront the possible disgrace of having adopted and acted on false instead of true principles. Free trade before them had been an idea; they made it a policy. Their action formed a turning-point in the commercial history of our country, and a short review of so stirring an episode cannot fail, we think, to prove interesting to a numerous class of readers.

We propose in the following pages to describe the struggles which marked the contest between the advocates and the adversaries of the free-trade system—to depict the men who took leading parts in it—to trace the motives and influences by which they were governed—to relate their alternate defeats and successes—to indicate the contemporaneous events which respectively assisted or impeded their efforts—and finally, after commemorating the triumph of the free-trade party, to inquire carefully and impartially into the substantial results of that victory as regards the prosperity and progress of the nation.

A political revolution is none the less real or the less important because it is bloodless; and the same interest which attaches to those armed conflicts which decide the fate of a campaign ought surely to attach to the intellectual encounters that decide the fate of a momentous political measure. A parliamentary debate is a battle in which, as in other battles, numbers generally prevail, but in which good generalship, tact, the eloquent exposition of earnest convictions, witty and suggestive allusions, and impressive appeals sometimes produce an immediate effect, while they always exercise more or less sway over the issue of subsequent struggles. And the results obtained in the parliamentary arena have generally wielded a far wider and more permanent influence over the future destinies of the country than those obtained in the battle-field.

In 1824 the fiscal regulations by which our commerce with the world was controlled and restricted stood as follows:— 1. There was hardly an article

1824. obtainable from abroad that was admissible here without the payment of import duties, always heavy, sometimes excessive, and in certain cases all but prohibitory. It mattered not whether it was a raw material or a manufactured product, whether it was an article of luxury or of universal consumption, whether it came in masses, like cotton, or in driblets, like orchilla—everything foreign which an Englishman might use was withheld from him till its cost had been enhanced by a customs' duty. The tariff list of the United Kingdom formed a tolerably complete dictionary of all the products of human industry.

To assess and collect these duties custom-houses were established in every part of the kingdom, down to the smallest fishing hamlet. At an expense which, in many cases, exceeded the sum collected, a multitudinous host was maintained of custom-house functionaries—commissioners, controllers, clerks, officers, examiners, collectors, &c. &c. To evade the duties and defraud the revenue, smuggling was adopted as a professional vocation by numbers of hardy men, who would have shrunk from any other form of lawlessness, and whose illicit practices were not only condoned, but abetted, by the many thousands who, directly or indirectly, dealt with them. A fleet of revenue cutters and an army of revenue officers, coast-guards, &c., were, at an enormous expense, employed to suppress smuggling and smugglers; but though frequent conflicts took place and much blood was shed, the object was not attained, and the contraband trade continued to flourish till extirpated by the more gentle and more effective process of fiscal reform.

2. In 1824 foreign wheat was totally prohibited from entering the United Kingdom until the average price throughout the country had reached 70s. per quarter. When the price exceeded that figure importation was allowed at a high duty, decreasing to 5s. 2d. per quarter when the current price reached 85s. per quarter. This Corn Law, which was enacted in 1822, under Lord Liverpool's administration, was bad enough, since it gave the landlords a monopoly of the wheat trade up to 70s. per quarter, and afforded no effectual relief till the price reached 85s. It was, however, rather less stringent than that which preceded it, for that totally prohibited the importation of foreign wheat until the current price in England had reached 80s. per quarter. That price for wheat meant something like 1s. 4d. per quartern loaf.

This earlier Corn Law had been passed in 1815, and no wonder that at the time of its being enacted popular indignation was excited to its utmost. Riotous assemblages had to be dispersed by armed force, and the House of Commons itself had to be protected by the soldiery, when the third reading of the Bill was voted by a large majority. This harsh measure, which took from the nation to give to a class, soon produced its inevitable results. Two or three deficient harvests successively occurred; and the price of wheat rose to 103s. per quarter in December, 1816, to 104s. in January, and to 112s. 8d. in June, 1817.

Of course, these extravagant prices and the admission duty free attracted enormous supplies from abroad; but from want of previous organisation for

1824. purchase and shipment, the supplies arrived slowly and tardily when the demand was intense, and poured in with superfluous abundance when it slackened. On the other hand, by the time that the country was fairly flooded with foreign wheat the tide began to turn: a cycle of good harvests set in, and prices underwent a heavy fall. The average price for 1821 was 56s. per quarter, and in December, 1821, the price fell to 38s. 8d. What trade—indeed what country—could prosper under the recurrence of such extravagant fluctuations as these in the price of food? In 1817 hundreds of thousands of the working classes were brought to the brink of starvation by wheat at 112s. per quarter; in 1821, thousands of farmers were brought to absolute ruin by wheat at 39s. per quarter, their rents having been fixed on the basis of high prices. An unnatural and unblessed state of things truly, since under it, if the nation enjoyed plenty, the farmers perished; and in order that the latter should prosper it was necessary that the people should partially starve.

The depression reached its acme at the commencement of 1822, and agricultural distress was one of the main topics of the king's speech at the opening of Parliament on the 5th of February of that year. With the double view of assisting the agriculturists, by retaining some duty, even at high prices, and of favouring the consumers, by allowing foreign importation to commence (under high duties) at 70s. per quarter, instead of 80s. as before, Lord Liverpool introduced the Corn Law Act of 1822. Strangely enough, this Act, which in 1828 was superseded by another, never came into actual operation at all; for prices throughout that interval did not reach 70s., and no importation of foreign wheat took place. It was this law—a law which barred imports except under a contingency that did not arise, and was therefore in practice prohibitory—that governed the corn trade in 1824.

3. Under the Navigation Act in force at the period from which we start, viz., in 1824, foreign commodities could only be imported in British ships, or in ships of the country from which the goods were exported, or of which the goods were the produce, and the colonial trade was entirely confined to the medium of British ships. Stringently as these laws operated in favour of the British ship-owner, they were mild in comparison with the Navigation Laws as they existed previous to 1815. Then the restriction extended to exports. No British goods could be exported except in British ships. Naturally enough, foreign nations retaliated, and the loss and annoyance to all parties were incalculable. Thus British ships conveyed our manufactures to America, and had to return in ballast, while American ships conveyed cotton to Liverpool, and had also to return empty. Could absurdity and wastefulness go farther? Two sets of ships were employed to perform one voyage! However, in 1815, by a convention with the United States, those disabilities were removed on both sides, and gradually similar arrangements were made with other countries.

But in every other respect the old Navigation Laws were upheld in all their exclusiveness, and were in 1824 regarded by the majority of the people as the Palladium of our maritime supremacy.

1824. Such, then, was the position in 1824 of our fiscal ordinances in regard to our commercial intercourse with other nations. It will be observed that there was not a single avenue through which the produce of foreign labour could obtain admittance into this country without the payment of a heavy toll. Every device was resorted to in order to induce the foreigner to buy of us, and to prevent us from buying of him. This was called "maintaining the balance of trade in our favour." But England was by no means the only country that pursued that delusive phantom, "the balance of trade." All other countries used the same means for obtaining the same end. All sought to sell much and to buy little—to accomplish, in fact, a sheer impossibility. It would have been just as reasonable to suppose that the distance from point A to point B being ten miles, it might only be six miles from point B to point A; thus giving a "balance of distance" of four miles in favour of B.

The process of curtailing purchases from abroad was easy enough, and it was adopted by all nations alike. It consisted simply in prohibiting, or checking by heavy duties, the admission of foreign goods. But how, at the same time, to prevent that very process from curtailing sales to the foreigner—that was the insoluble problem which grave statesmen vainly set themselves to solve. Each nation hoped that this imaginary "balance of trade" would be paid to it in gold. Everybody fondly and foolishly looked to receive an annual tribute of bullion from everybody else. Of course, this dream was never realised, and never could be. These modern Tantali held forth their bowls to receive the golden showers, but the bowls never reached their lips otherwise than empty. The only practical issue of the successful endeavour to buy little was the undesirable result of selling just as little ; and thus, the substantial benefits which free commercial intercourse would have conferred on all were discarded in the vain and absurd attempt of each country to obtain some special advantage at the expense of the rest.

England had at that period everything that a nation could ever hope to enjoy in the way of restrictive policy. If ample protection could make a people happy and flourishing, we ought then to have been at the zenith of our prosperity. But far from that, the condition of the people was deplorable. They suffered from low wages and dear bread, from bad laws harshly administered, and from frequent, sudden, and injurious fluctuations in the demand for their labour. Political discontent, revealing itself in occasional rioting rudely repressed by violence and bloodshed, was rife throughout the country. But in the Legislature its voice was little heeded, for it was not the people, but a class, which was then represented in Parliament.

It is not surprising that while the attention of both people and Government was engrossed by the demand for, and the resistance to, large political reforms, the advocates for an improved fiscal system met with few listeners. Amid the din and clatter of political conflicts, the doctrines of free trade were urged in vain by those who had studied the subject.

And although the principles propounded by a small band of enlightened inquirers were supported

1824. in Parliament by such men as Canning, Huskisson, Robinson, and Wallace, no measure involving their adoption was passed till the session of 1823. In January of that year Mr. Huskisson was appointed President of the Board of Trade. That eminent statesman, whose untimely death in 1830 was an immense loss to the cause of free trade, made the first breach in our Navigation Laws by a Bill, which he carried through the House in July, 1823, enacting that all duties and drawbacks should be levied and allowed equally on goods, whether in British or foreign vessels. This was the thin end of the wedge, and a very thin end it was.

In the following year he struck a heavier blow at the protective system. Up to that time all foreign silk manufactures had been totally prohibited. It was not a question of heavy import duties; they were not admitted into the United Kingdom at all. The force of protection could no farther go. It was the despotism of monopoly, tempered only by the smuggler. Joseph Hume on one occasion amused the House of Commons by flourishing his silk bandanna handkerchief before them, exclaiming, "Here is a foreign ware that is totally prohibited. Nearly every one of you has a similar illicit article in his pocket. So much for your prohibition!"

How did this highly favoured manufacture thrive? Its chief seat was then, not as now Coventry and Macclesfield, but Spitalfields, London; and that district was, nevertheless, one of the poorest, the most frequently distressed, and the most turbulent in the metropolis. It was quite a common occurrence for thousands of

Spitalfields weavers, when their trade was depressed, as it frequently was in spite of protection, to parade the streets in bands, clamorously demanding alms. Rioting was with them a favourite amusement. At one time, fancying themselves injured by the fashion that had set in of using printed calicoes for female dresses, gangs of these silk-weavers went about throwing corrosive liquids on cotton dresses, and even brutally tearing them from the wearers' backs. At another time, under the impression that numbers of Irishmen had recently arrived in London for the purpose of working at under-prices, they assembled in crowds, and proceeded to Brick Lane, Whitechapel, where they attacked a house in which Irishmen were supposed to be harboured, and demolished it, at the expense of one death and many wounded. Such were the freaks of these spoiled children of protection.

Mr. Huskisson, on the 5th of March, 1824, proposed (and the measure was carried) that the prohibition on the importation of silk manufactures should cease on the 5th of July, 1826, that the duties on raw silk should be largely reduced, and those on thrown silk lessened one-half. In his speech he introduced the following argument, on which he laid great stress:—"The prohibitory duties," he said, "which have been maintained with respect to the silk trade have had the effect—to the shame of England be it spoken—of leaving us far behind our neighbours in this branch of industry. We have witnessed that chilling and benumbing effect which is always sure to be felt when no genius is called into action, and when we are rendered indifferent to exertion by the indolent

1825, 1826. security of a prohibitory system." Everybody knows how largely our silk manufactures have expanded since the alteration.

No doubt that other fiscal changes of a similar tendency would have been subsequently introduced by a Ministry of which Canning and Huskisson were influential members, but the pressure of events rendered it impossible. The years 1825 and 1826 are painfully memorable for the occurrence of one of the severest commercial panics by which this country has ever been visited. It sprang from the same old cause, reaction, that has always led to the same result. The inflated prosperity and reckless speculations of 1824-5 led to the financial catastrophe of 1825-6. Seven London bankers and sixty-seven country banks stopped payment. The number of bankruptcies in 1826 was nearly 2,600. People, mistrusting paper money, "ran for gold," and the bullion in the Bank of England was reduced to £1,300,000. As somebody said, the country was within twenty-four hours of barter. Immense numbers of working men were thrown out of employment, and the distress was universal.

At length the nation emerged from the crisis, but it was not in such times that attention could be bestowed on the question of fiscal reform.

CHAPTER II.

(1827 to 1839.)

New Corn Law of 1828 merely a slight Shift in the Sliding Scale—Catholic Emancipation in 1829—Reform Bill in 1832—Lord Melbourne's Administration—Financial Crisis of 1837—Accession of Queen Victoria—Manchester Anti-Corn-Law Association formed in 1838—Mr. Villiers' Motions on the Corn Laws in February and March, 1839—Sir Robert Peel's unsuccessful Attempt to Form a Ministry.

IN 1827 Lord Liverpool's Administration, which had lasted fifteen years, was broken up by his severe illness, and George Canning, who succeeded him as Prime Minister, closed his brilliant career a few months later. The premature death of this eminent man excited universal sympathy and regret. Eloquent and witty but flippant in his youth, he had become, as he advanced in life and experience, earnest and wise as well as witty and eloquent. Time seemed to have ripened and mellowed his powers, and England had looked to him, when at the age of fifty-seven he became Prime Minister, as one of her guiding spirits for many a future year.

In 1828 the reins of government were assumed by the Duke of Wellington, and among his colleagues were Peel and Huskisson. The only measure passed during that year which had any direct relation to our subject was a remodelled sliding scale of corn duties, under which the import duty on wheat was to be 25s. 8d. per quarter when the average price in England was under 62s.; 24s. 8d. when from 62s. to 63s.; and so gradually reduced to 1s. when the average

1828—
1832.
price was 73s. and upwards. This Act was passed on the 15th of July, 1828.

During the ensuing few years the public mind was pre-occupied and absorbed by two questions of paramount importance, Catholic emancipation and Parliamentary reform. The discussions and struggles through which the first had to pass extended over the two years 1828 and 1829, and the final settlement of the second was not effected till July, 1832. In December of that year Parliament was dissolved, and a general election took place under entirely novel conditions, namely, under the provisions of the Reform Bill.

This is not the place to refer at any length to the contrast which the actual constitution of the new Parliament presented to the fears of the Conservative and the hopes of the Democratic party. Instead of the truculent and ferocious monster that many anticipated, the reformed House of Commons turned out to be quite a tame and well-behaved body—rather coy and bashful than forward or fierce. It passed two very important measures: the abolition of slavery in the British colonies, at the cost of £20,000,000 by way of indemnity, and the Poor-Law Amendment Bill, both of which were exceedingly creditable to the new Legislature.

But so little of the revolutionary spirit did it collectively evince, that within less than two years of its first meeting, a Conservative Ministry became possible. In November, 1834, Sir Robert Peel and the Duke of Wellington came into power, though only for a short time. A dissolution ensued, and a second reformed Parliament restored Lord Melbourne and the Whigs to their ministerial functions in April, 1835.

These rapid shiftings of the political scenes were very unfavourable to the introduction of legislative improvements, and the only large measure passed in 1835 was the Reform of Municipal Corporations.

Meanwhile the population was yearly increasing, while the productive power of the land remained unaltered. More food was being wanted, but no more food was being raised. In obedience to the law of supply and demand, the price of wheat kept gradually advancing. Of course, the pressure was less severe with good, and more severe with bad harvests, but the general tendency was towards an increased demand, which was not met by an increased supply. It was evident that the disproportion would become greater every year, and public opinion was rapidly being aroused to the injurious operation of the existing corn laws and of the system of restrictive import duties generally.

But the year 1836 passed away without any direct 1836. action in Parliament on matters connected with free trade. The very abundant harvest of 1835 had given the people comparatively cheap bread, and the voice of complaint was hushed for a time. Reflective men were well aware that this was the transitory lull due to an exceptional circumstance, not the settled repose arising from healthy political conditions. That scarcity and high prices would soon prevail again was as certain as it was that exuberant crops are an exception, not a rule. But now, the effects of the taxes on

1836. food being for a moment unfelt, they were for that moment forgotten by the impulsive multitude.

Meanwhile the Government of Lord Melbourne passed some excellent secondary measures. The Tithe Commutation Act, that for allowing counsel to prisoners, the Act for the general registration of births, deaths, and marriages, the reduction (from 4d. to 1d.) of the stamp on newspapers, and a large abatement in the paper duty, were all of them decided steps in the path of progress. The latter measure especially was fruitful in useful results, as it placed newspapers within the reach of a far greater number than heretofore, and thus not only promoted political discussion, but by promulgating the knowledge of historical and statistical facts, afforded it a wider and sounder basis. By multiplying the points of contact between the people and their teachers, it largely increased the influence of the latter, and lightened the task of substituting truth for error.

The prosperity which prevailed during the greater part of this year gave way towards its close. Not only did the harvest of 1836 prove deficient, and a considerable rise in the price of wheat ensue in autumn, but a commercial crisis was impending. It was the old, old story. Prosperity led to over-speculation, and over-speculation to collapse. The storm did not, however, burst immediately, and we shall have occasion to allude to it further on. But there were various indications and warnings of its approach, and the year set in gloom.

1837. In the spring of 1837 the commercial depression to which we have alluded became more urgent, and resulted in heavy failures in London and the great provincial centres of trade, Manchester, Liverpool, and Glasgow. At last, in June, the climax was reached by the failure of three great American houses, viz., Wilson & Co., Wildes & Co., and Wiggin & Co. (the three W's, as they were familiarly termed), with liabilities to an enormous amount. Things after this began to mend, but not till severe distress had been encountered by many thousands of the working classes.

In March an attempt was made by Mr. Clay to obtain from Parliament, not the repeal, but a modification of the Corn Laws. He moved for the adoption of a fixed impost of 10s. per quarter on wheat, in lieu of the sliding scale of duties. Only 89 members voted for his motion, while 223 voted against it. Of his 89 supporters, ten, including Lords Howick and Morpeth, Sir George Grey, Sir Henry Parnell, and Mr. Labouchere, were connected with the Government.

If this was the reception given to a fixed duty of 10s. per quarter, what kind of favour might be expected for a proposition of total repeal? If all that a minority can do is, as Mr. Disraeli has asserted, to convert itself as quickly as it can into a majority, here was a signal opportunity for performing this difficult feat. How successfully it was achieved will be duly shown in the course of these pages.

On the 20th June the King, William the Fourth, died. Succeeding as he did one of the worst, and preceding as he did one of the best of our English sovereigns, his memory bears a neutral tint, and is

1837. associated in our minds with few vices and with few virtues. The one event which gave a distinctive character to his reign was the passing of the Reform Bill, and he is entitled to the negative merit of not having offered any obstinate resistance to the measure. Queen Victoria, at the age of eighteen, assumed the government of this mighty empire, whose sway extends over a large proportion of the total population of this globe, and which is the mother-land of the innumerable English-speaking people who are rapidly replenishing the waste places of the earth. It is under her auspicious reign—her hereditary presidency of the great English commonwealth—that our country has prospered and progressed beyond all precedent. That much yet remains to be done—that mountains of bad legislation have still to be removed, and valleys of deficient legislation to be made good—is undoubtedly true, but we feel by no means disheartened at the task that remains, when we see how much of it has already been accomplished.

The general election that necessarily followed the inauguration of the new reign did not much alter the relative strength of the Ministerialists and their opponents, and Lord Melbourne's Administration continued to receive for a time the lukewarm support of a moderate majority. That this majority, such as it was, should have been returned was rather owing to the immense popularity of the Queen than to any general appreciation of the merits of the Ministry. Their course, while it was mainly in the right direction, was too slow to please one party, and too liberal in its tendencies to please the other. They offended the Conservatives by what they did, and a large section of their own supporters by what they did not do.

The attention of Parliament was chiefly directed during the session of 1838 to the settlement of the Canadian question, to the exclusion of all but unimportant domestic measures. Meanwhile, two parties in the State, quite opposed to each other, were slowly gathering strength and undermining that of the Ministry. The Conservatives desired to slacken, the Free-traders to accelerate, the pace of our political progress. A public dinner was given to Sir Robert Peel by 313 members of the House of Commons, which exhibited the great strength of the Tory party, made public the accession to its ranks of Lord Stanley and his followers, and showed that the time was not far distant when a struggle would be made for the possession of Ministerial power.

On the other hand, the fiscal reformers were equally active in marshalling and organising their forces. It chanced that in September of this year, Dr. Bowring, on his return from a commercial mission abroad, was passing through Manchester, when he was asked to assist at a suddenly improvised meeting, called together on the spur of the moment by a private circular, which Mr. A. Prentice, the originator of the idea, issued to about 100 gentlemen. Of these, 60 responded to the summons. Dr. Bowring addressed them in an interesting and animated speech, in the course of which he vehemently denounced the Corn Laws. The meeting displayed great enthusiasm, and a sudden proposition to form an Anti-Corn-

1838. Law Association in Manchester was warmly received. Accordingly, seven gentlemen met on the subsequent Monday, who, after canvassing a few days for members and subscriptions, were enabled to publish in the *Manchester Times* of the 13th October, 1838, a list of thirty-eight gentlemen, as "Provisional Committee of the Manchester Anti-Corn-Law Association." In this first list appears the name of John Bright, of Rochdale. The week after, thirty-one more gentlemen were announced as forming an addition to the provisional committee. In this second list appears the name of Richard Cobden, of Mosley Street.

Subscriptions poured in liberally, and the committee set vigorously to work. A young medical student, Mr. A. W. Paulton, had been found at a previous meeting to possess the requisite qualifications of talent, information, and energy, and he was invited to deliver a lecture on the 25th October, at the Manchester Corn Exchange. The room was filled to overflowing; the committee occupied the platform, and Mr. J. B. Smith was placed in the chair. The lecture was impressively delivered and enthusiastically received. From many other towns requests were soon made for lectures by Mr. Paulton, for which purpose the committee made arrangements with him, and this early missionary in the cause of free trade entered on an active and successful career.

The next step taken was to secure the co-operation of the Manchester Chamber of Commerce. A requisition to the president of that institution, G. Wood, M.P. for Kendal, was numerously signed, and in accordance with its tenor, a general meeting of the members was held on the 13th of December. A petition to the House of Commons for the repeal of the existing Corn Laws was proposed for the adoption of the meeting. But to the thorough Free-traders, represented by J. B. Smith and Richard Cobden, it did not appear sufficiently vigorous and explicit. At their suggestion, therefore, the meeting was adjourned for a week. At the adjourned meeting, which was numerously attended, another petition, of a decided character, which had been drawn up by Mr. Cobden, was proposed by him, and carried by a large majority. The discussions, which lasted five hours at each meeting, were conducted with much ability, and full reports were read with interest both in the metropolis and in the provinces.

On the 10th January, 1839, the Anti-Corn-Law Association held a meeting, with a view to devise the mode of conducting their operations in the most efficient manner. Before arranging a plan of campaign, it was requisite, however, to ascertain what amount of funds they might command. The answer was soon given; £1,800 was subscribed by the meeting on the spot, and the subscriptions amounted by the 9th of February to £6,136. A series of other meetings, including a public dinner given on the 22nd of January to Mr. C. P. Villiers, M.P., and several other members of Parliament who had voted for Mr. Villiers' annual motion for the repeal of the Corn Laws, and which was attended by 800 guests, occupied the time and attention of the association continuously till the end of the month.

The chief practical results of their labours were to

1839. urge the formation of Anti-Corn-Law Associations in every commercial town throughout the kingdom, and to resolve that delegates should be appointed by each of these associations, who were to meet in London (at Brown's Hotel, Westminster) on Monday, 4th February next ensuing, to form a Central Board at the opening of Parliament. The association also appointed a Permanent Council, which was divided into various committees. The Executive Committee, on which devolved the main burden, and which continued its functions when the association merged into the League, consisted of twelve members, whose names deserve to be recorded. We give them at foot.*

The meeting of the various delegates appointed in accordance with the resolution referred to assembled in London on the 4th February. Mr. Villiers and other members of the House met and conferred with them, and it was arranged that at the earliest possible date Mr. Villiers should move in the House of Commons that evidence be heard at the bar of the House in support of the petitions against the Corn Laws.

The Queen's Speech made no reference to the Corn Law question; but Mr. Wood, who was selected by

---

* The Executive Committee to the Manchester Anti-Corn-Law Association appointed in January, 1839, consisted of the following gentlemen:—* W. R. Callender, James Chapman, Walter Clarke, * Richard Cobden, George Dixon, Peter Eckersley, * William Evans, James Howie, Edward Hall, * Archibald Prentice, * William Rawson, * George Wilson. They were subsequently elected to form the Executive Committee of the National Anti-Corn-Law League. When, after seven years' labours, the League dissolved in 1846, the six gentlemen named above to whose name an astcrisk is prefixed were still members of the Executive Committee.

Ministers to second the Address, treated the subject in a way that greatly displeased his constituents. As President of the Manchester Chamber of Commerce, he had just sent up a petition depicting the state of trade in the gloomiest colours, and ascribing the depression to the operation of the Corn Laws. In his speech he reversed the picture, and, presumably in grateful return to the Ministers who had appointed him to his honourable function, gave a glowing and exaggerated account of the prosperous condition of our commerce and manufactures. Sir Robert Peel rapidly took advantage of this admission, and made an effective speech, the burden of which was, "Why press for a change in the Corn Laws, since under their operation you enjoy such prosperity?" Hot-and-cold-blowing Mr. Wood secured the sarcastic applause of the Protectionists, but that was a poor compensation for the indignant protests of his colleagues and constituents. Not many days after his ill-advised speech he had ceased to be President, or even Director of the Manchester Chamber of Commerce.

It was now determined to bring the question once more to the test of a formal division in the House of Commons, and on the 19th February, Mr. Villiers moved "That J. B. Smith, R. H. Greg, and others be heard at the bar of this House, by their witnesses, agents, or counsel, in support of their petition, presented to the House on the 15th inst., complaining of the operation of the Corn Laws." After a short but animated debate, the motion was rejected by 361 votes against 172. Three Cabinet Ministers voted in the minority: Lord Morpeth, Sir J. C. Hobhouse, and

1839. C. P. Thomson. On the adverse side we find the names of Lord Palmerston and Lord John Russell.

This result, far from unexpected, rather stimulated than discouraged the delegates. They met the next morning with a renewed determination to continue the contest with unabated vigour. Richard Cobden, who had rapidly advanced to the front rank, and was already hailed as one of the most distinguished leaders of the movement, addressed the meeting in a buoyant spirit. "The delegates," he cried, "had offered to instruct the House; the House had refused to be instructed. But the House must be instructed; and the most unexceptionable and effectual way will be by instructing the nation."

The delegates left London for their respective homes, but were soon called upon for renewed action, and they were summoned to meet in the rooms of the Manchester Association on the 7th March. Accordingly, on that day there assembled at Manchester a numerous body of gentlemen delegated by and representing the following twenty-two important towns: Birmingham, Bolton, Bradford, Burnley, Derby, Dundee, Edinburgh, Glasgow, Halifax, Huddersfield, Hull, Kendal, Lancaster, Leeds, Leicester, Liverpool, London, Manchester, Nottingham, Sowerby Bridge, Warrington, and Wigan. Mr. R. H. Greg was called to the chair, and a number of strong resolutions were passed. Among others was the following: "That the delegates having learned that on Tuesday, the 12th inst., Mr. Villiers brings on a motion in the House of Commons, for a Committee of the whole House on the subject of the Corn Laws, do forthwith adjourn to

London, and that the first meeting take place at Brown's Hotel, Palace Yard, at eleven o'clock on Tuesday morning, the 12th inst." On the evening of that day, March 12th, Mr. Villiers moved in the House of Commons, "That it should resolve itself into a Committee of the whole House to take into consideration the Act, 9 Geo. IV., regulating the importation of foreign corn." The question was debated for five nights, and on a division being taken, there were 195 votes in favour of the motion, and 342 against it; majority, 147.

After so decided an expression of parliamentary opinion, there was clearly nothing to be gained by the presence of the provincial delegates in London. But before dispersing, they held one more meeting on the 20th March, at which they laid the foundation of that body which afterwards exercised so mighty an influence over public opinion. An address was drawn up which recommended, among other measures, "the formation of a permanent union, to be called the Anti-Corn-Law League, composed of all the towns and districts represented in the delegation, and as many others as might be induced to form Anti-Corn-Law Associations and to join the League." They further resolved that the central office of the League should be established in Manchester, that at least £5,000 should be raised to defray expenses, and that the meeting should adjourn subject to the call of the Manchester Anti-Corn-Law Association.

The next step was to enter upon the task which Richard Cobden had suggested, that of "instructing the nation." Accordingly, in April, the first number

1839. was published in Manchester of the "Anti-Corn-Law Circular," which, as the organ of the movement, rapidly obtained a circulation of 15,000 copies. Besides this publication, which was issued weekly, numerous pamphlets such as "Facts for Farmers," Mr. Villiers' speech, Mr. Poulett Thomson's speech, &c. &c., we recirculated in tens of thousands. And, as many might be willing to listen who might not care to read, those were reached by means of lecturers who were engaged to deliver addresses in all parts of the kingdom. Messrs. Paulton, Sydney Smith, Acland, and others, orally impressed the doctrines of Free Trade on the minds of hundreds of thousands, and although occasionally obstructed in their task, sometimes by Chartists and sometimes by Tories, they generally met with an appreciative reception.

Meanwhile the Melbourne Administration had exhibited increasing weakness, and the majority in the House of Commons by which it was supported had so dwindled that, on the 7th May, Lord John Russell announced that Ministers, not having such support from the House as would enable them to carry on the public business with efficiency, had resigned office. Sir Robert Peel was called in to form a new Administration, but in consequence of his having insisted on some Household changes to which the Queen objected as "contrary to usage and repugnant to her feelings," his attempt to form a Ministry proved abortive, and the Melbourne Administration, after a week's intermission, resumed office. The majority of the nation sympathised with Her Majesty's views, and it was the opinion of many that Sir R. Peel was not sorry to have a pretext for evading a premature accession to power, in view of the many difficulties which a Conservative Ministry would have to encounter in the existing state of public opinion.

On the 5th July the Ministers brought forward the Budget for the year. To the common apprehension, a Budget is merely a dry, dreary, perplexing array of figures, only tolerable if it results in the remission of taxation, but absolutely repulsive and nauseating if it leads to an increase of burdens. In the present instance, however, although the Budget did exhibit a deficit, there was a redeeming point in it which renders it memorable in the annals of social progress. This was the virtual adoption of Rowland Hill's Penny Postage scheme. It required considerable moral courage on the part of the Ministry to initiate this measure. It threatened a heavy increase of the large deficit in the revenue that already existed. It was vehemently opposed, and was pronounced to be a chimerical and ruinous innovation by nearly every Post Office official. Sir Robert Peel and Mr. Goulburn led the opposition to it in the House of Commons. Even the Liberals were not unanimous in its support, and although the Free-trade party were its ardent advocates, so advanced a Whig as the Rev. Sydney Smith stigmatised the measure as "nonsensical."

It was, however, passed, and resulted in such a development of the written intercourse between man and man as immeasurably exceeded the most sanguine expectations of its originators. It was the removal of a heavy tax on the interchange of thought. And even in a financial aspect, it eventually proved a huge suc-

1839. cess. It is to English statesmen that the glory is due of having inaugurated one of those sovereign improvements that give an impulse to progress all the world over. By foreign governments it was at first sneered at as a visionary project, then wondered at as a not hopeless experiment, and finally adopted everywhere as a substantial success. It is in the same way that we have seen English statesmen inaugurate from *à priori* convictions the free-trade system, and that we now see that system going through just the same three phases as Post-office reform with our friends abroad. It has gone through the first, and its success with us takes it clean out of the category of a "visionary project." It is now viewed by foreign governments as in its second stage, and they are already rather shaken in their previous idea of the hopelessness of the experiment. They are beginning curiously to inquire whether or not there can be anything in it. It will not be long before they reach the third stage, and adopt free trade as thoroughly as they adopted cheap postage, to the incalculable benefit of the people over whose welfare they are supposed to preside.

CHAPTER III

(1840 to 1841.)

The Anti-Corn-Law Associations take measures to "instruct the Nation"—Joseph Hume's Committee of Inquiry—The Queen's Marriage—Labours of the Anti-Corn-Law League.

DURING the ensuing year, 1840, no great overt progress was made in the cause of free trade, and the

Parliamentary majority against it was as large as ever. But throughout the country a spirit of inquiry was roused, and the conviction was rapidly gaining ground with the great and usually inert mass of the public, that the welfare of the kingdom required the repeal of the Corn Laws. The system adopted of "instructing the nation" was bearing its fruits, and through the unremitting efforts of the central body of Free-traders at Manchester, the great bulk of the English people, slow to move, but resistless when moved, were at first stirred to thought, and soon after stirred to action, on a subject of such vital importance to every household in the country. The leaders of the movement were adepts in the art of converting a minority into a majority. To overcome Parliamentary obstruction, they addressed themselves to the Parliamentary constituencies. They appealed from the public representatives to the public conscience. To outward observation, the Protectionists were as strong as ever; Whigs and Tories, at mortal strife on most other subjects, united their forces to combat fiscal reform, and Parliament exhibited no symptom of a change of attitude on that subject. But, silently, steadily, surely, public opinion was becoming largely leavened by the new doctrines, and public opinion is a force of which even autocracies recognise the power, and which in representative governments is irresistible.

Let us take a rapid glance at the tactics of the Free-traders at this juncture. A meeting of the delegates was summoned to Manchester, where a grand banquet was to be held on the 13th January. To accommodate the expected guests, as there was no hall in the town

1840. nearly large enough for the purpose, a temporary pavilion was erected, 150 feet in length and 105 in width. There were twenty-five tables, with seats for 3,800 persons. By a strange coincidence, the site of the erection was St. Peter's Field, the very spot where, twenty-one years before, a meeting, held for the purpose of petitioning Parliament for Reform and the repeal of the Corn Laws, was brutally and illegally swept away by a cavalry charge, with the result of six persons killed and upwards of seventy wounded. Such coincidences and contrasts afford valuable landmarks whereby to measure the progress of social and political improvement.

The banquet was eminently successful, and, large as was the number admitted, larger still was the number of those whose demands for tickets had to be refused. Mr. J. B. Smith, the president of the Anti-Corn-Law Association, occupied the chair, and he was supported by twenty-six members of Parliament. Among these were C. P. Villiers, Daniel O'Connell, Sir De Lacy Evans, and many other celebrities. The next day followed another banquet, and 5,000 working men sat down to dine together in this noble hall, while the gallery was occupied by their wives and daughters. On both occasions excellent speeches were delivered by Cobden, O'Connell, Villiers, and many others. The utmost order, harmony, and enthusiasm prevailed, and the ample reports given by the metropolitan and provincial press, both of what was done and what was said at this important gathering, attracted much attention and excited much interest throughout the country.

On the 24th March the delegates met in London by appointment, and deputations were formed to wait on Ministers and on influential members of Parliament. On the 27th, a deputation of 200 delegates, among whom were a dozen men whose aggregate yearly expenditure in wages exceeded £1,000,000, waited on Lord Melbourne at the Colonial Office. They got very little out of that clever, cool, careless Minister. He shielded himself behind the reciprocity plea: "Foreign nations would not relax their protective duties. If they would consult their own interest it might be otherwise, but the general opinion of the world was against free trade. To give all first was not the way to commence negotiations for reciprocal advantages. There could be no question that their principle was right; but nations did not always see their own interest." Finally, he said that he could not pledge himself. He acknowledged the respectability of the deputation, but the Government had left the matter to the House of Commons.

Similar interviews took place, attended by similarly unsatisfactory results, with Sir Robert Peel, Sir Jas. Graham, and Mr. Baring (Chancellor of the Exchequer). The leading members of the deputations—Richard Cobden, Joseph Sturge, J. B. Smith, and others—were in turns argumentative, pathetic, supplicatory, and indignant; but the impassive official mind, chiefly intent on not committing itself to anything, received their remarks in that coolly-collected, punctiliously-civil, and mildly-sarcastic manner, which provokes, while it does not justify, resentment. A newly-made Minister, "caught young," may occasionally be lured

1840. into dangerous promises and admissions; but the mature, case-hardened statesman neither promises nor admits anything, and tenderly manipulates his deputation so as to dismiss it either indignant without any discernible pretext for complaint, or satisfied without any substantial reason for its satisfaction.

On Wednesday, the 1st April, Mr. Villiers moved "That the House resolve itself into a Committee of the whole House, to take into consideration the Act of George IV. regulating the importation of foreign corn." After three nights' debate, it was by some technical manœuvre adjourned *sine die*, and the motion became a dropped order. It was renewed by Mr. Villiers on the 26th May, but although the vital importance of the question was freely admitted, and although the aggregate petitions presented in its favour embodied a million and a half of signatures, the speeches of its supporters were received with such incessant shouts of "Divide, divide," that a division was forced on the very first night, and there appeared 300 votes against and 177 for it, showing a majority of 123.

Clearly, then, it was not from this Parliament that any concession was to be looked for. It was not from a Whig House of Commons supporting a Whig Ministry that measures of relief would come. Indeed, even if the Administration had felt it their duty and had screwed up their courage to move in the matter, they were too weak to have insured success. A junction between the landlords of their own party and Sir Robt. Peel's followers would have left them in a hopeless minority. It was in the next Parliament, and therefore in the electors on whom its constitution depended, that the Free-trade party must place their hopes, and they accordingly redoubled their efforts to educate and influence public opinion.

In the meantime that earnest and indefatigable reformer, Joseph Hume, had on the 5th of May obtained a Select Committee of the House of Commons, "to inquire into the several duties levied upon imports into the United Kingdom, and how far those duties are for protection to similar articles, the produce of this country or of the British possessions abroad, or whether the duties are for revenue alone." How such a committee came to be appointed by a Protectionist majority in the House of Commons, may well be a matter of surprise. No doubt, by many, its import and meaning was not understood; by some, the effect of its investigations was under-rated; and by, perhaps, not a few, it was considered that if the inquiry did lead to the abolition of protective duties on British manufactures, it would be a fitting punishment on those Manchester manufacturers for so pitilessly assailing the Corn Laws which protected the landowners. True, that these Manchester manufacturers had declared over and over again, that they did not want for themselves any protective duties whatever, that they disclaimed and repudiated them, and that those trades or callings which could not exist from their own intrinsic merits, and which required a national subvention to support them, not only contributed nothing to national wealth, but constituted a drain on the national resources. But these announcements were deemed by many Protectionists to be mere empty

1840. declamation. "Was it likely," they said, "that the manufacturers of cotton, woollen, linen, silken, and hardware goods would relinquish the advantage which import duties on foreign goods of the same kind gave them in the home market? No! let the war be carried into the enemy's territory. Make a raid on protection to British fabrics, and the British manufacturers would soon desist from their attack on protection to British land."

Whatever may have been the motives under the influence of which Mr. Hume's committee of inquiry was allowed, its appointment led to most important though slowly-developed results. It elicited from numerous experts and, among others, from such men as Macgregor, G. R. Porter (the able author of the "Progress of the Nation") and J. Deacon Hume, who had for forty-nine years been engaged at the Customs and at the Board of Trade, evidence utterly condemnatory of the prevailing system. That evidence went to show that while revenue duties give to Government what they take from the public, protective duties give what they take from the public to a limited number of private traders, and by so doing, divert capital and labour from remunerative to wasteful employment. It is difficult to over-estimate the result accruing from the labours of this Import Duties Committee. Their report at first attracted but little attention, but the facts were so striking, the reasoning so cogent, and the inferences so significant, that soon thoughtful and conscientious statesmen received from it fresh lights which largely modified their previous opinions.

Its influence was perceptible to some degree in the

Whig Budget of 1841, but was recognisable to a far greater extent in the fiscal improvements introduced soon afterwards by Sir Robert Peel. It was the first semi-official adoption of free-trade principles, and was somewhat the less obnoxious to the land-owners, as it bore on the entire range of protected articles and did not direct any separate or special attack on the Corn Laws.

On the 11th of August, Parliament was prorogued, and a barren Session came to an end. One of the chief events of the year was the marriage of the Queen with Prince Albert of Saxe-Coburg and Gotha, a marriage that proved singularly auspicious under every point of view, public and private. The bright exemplar of unclouded domestic happiness in the highest domestic circle—the Prince's prudent abstention from interference in party strife, coupled with his indefatigable labours in respect to art cultivation and social progress—his successful inauguration of the Great Exhibition—indeed, every act of his life attested how fortunate for the Queen and for the nation proved the choice that had been made of a Prince Consort.

The work which the Anti-Corn-Law League had set itself to do was done thoroughly and efficiently. All England was over-run by its emissaries. Wherever an assemblage could be collected, large or small, that were willing to listen, the League's lecturers, able and eloquent men, attended to address them. More than 800 lectures were delivered this season, chiefly in the English provinces, but partly also in Scotland, Ireland, and Wales. Public meetings without number were held on the subject of the Corn Laws throughout the

1840. country, many of them promoted, nearly all attended, by members of the League deputed for the purpose. Among the most active, laborious, and effective soldiers in this new crusade were Richard Cobden, J. Brooks, W. Rawson, A. Prentice, and L. Heyworth. The number of speeches these men delivered, the distances they travelled, the opposition which they encountered and generally overcame, the physical and mental strain they endured, the insults and obloquy with which they were frequently assailed, it were vain, if it were possible, to detail. It was only by such unflagging efforts that the victory could be won; it was only by enthusiasts in the cause that such efforts could be made. Let us exemplify the nature of the opposition which at these meetings the free-trade orators had to encounter.

On the 30th November a large public meeting was held at Warrington, at which Richard Cobden and three other members of the League were present. At this meeting Chartism was the disturbing element. Chartism, no longer heard of but only read of, was at that period to some extent a power in the State. Its sectaries contended that the country could never prosper until the following six measures were carried: 1, universal suffrage; 2, vote by ballot; 3, annual Parliaments; 4, division of the United Kingdom into equal electoral districts; 5, abolition of property qualification for members of Parliament; and 6, payment to members for their services. But not content with advocating these measures as means of political improvement, they insisted that these were the only means, and that all other measures devised or proposed for the good of the country were delusive and misleading, and were therefore to be resisted and obstructed. Their leaders, Feargus O'Connor, M.P., Oastler, Stephens, &c., viewed the Anti-Corn-Law movement with jealousy and dislike. It diverted the attention of the people from the Charter; and what would become of Chartism if bread were to be made cheap and the physical condition of the working classes improved? They therefore gave the cue to their followers, and at a great many of the meetings convened by the Anti-Corn-Law Associations, Chartists attended in greater or lesser number, and the proceedings were interrupted, and sometimes disorganised, by discordant noises, by adverse amendments, and occasionally even by a resort to physical force.

At the Warrington meeting to which we have referred, a number of Chartists were present, and one of them named Travis proposed an amendment in favour of the six points of the Charter, arguing that their immediate adoption would insure and embrace all necessary reforms, and that it was a waste of time to attend to mere subsidiary topics such as the Corn Law question. Besides, in his opinion, the repeal of the Corn Laws would throw land out of cultivation. To this Cobden replied in a speech so replete with clear and forcible argument, so abounding with illustrations that went "home to the business and bosoms" of the men, and in so temperate and even kindly a tone, that the meeting was entirely won over and all opposition was withdrawn.

Another meeting was held on the 21st December, at Macclesfield, the great seat of the silk manufac-

1840. turers. Here the opposition was based on local and personal interests. An apprehension prevailed lest free trade, by throwing the silk manufacture open to foreign competition, should work injury to both the masters and workmen of the place. Cobden and three other members attended as a deputation from the League. Their efforts were successful. After a long discussion, in which Cobden as usual distinguished himself, the meeting resulted in the formation of a local Anti-Corn-Law Association disclaiming all protection to native manufactures.

While one section of the League was doing missionary duty abroad, another was busily engaged at the Central Office in the work of spreading its doctrines by means of correspondence and publication. Every clergyman, every corporation, and every poor-law guardian in the kingdom received a special invitation to co-operate in the movement; the formation of Anti-Corn-Law Associations in every place where there was the slightest chance for one was suggested, urged, and promoted; upwards of 300,000 copies of "The Anti-Corn-Law Circular" had been issued, and innumerable tracts, &c., had been distributed. Truly the task of "instructing the nation" was being performed in an effective and vigorous fashion.

1841. Early in the spring of the year 1841, a series of public meetings took place in furtherance of the Anti-Corn-Law movement. On the 18th of February, the Manchester Anti-Corn-Law Association, one only, though a leading one, of the numerous associations throughout the kingdom which, combined, constituted the Anti-Corn-Law League, held a meeting under the

Presidency of J. B. Smith. A numerous committee was re-appointed, and the machinery which had already worked so powerfully on public opinion was strengthened and improved. On the 12th of March, the Manchester Chamber of Commerce met and adopted an able report presented by the directors " on the injurious effects of restrictions on trade, and the necessity of immediate changes in our commercial policy, as proved by the report and evidence of the Select Committee of the House of Commons on Import Duties, during the last Session of Parliament." This report was widely circulated in the form of a pamphlet, and in this shape attracted much attention. Thus was Joseph Hume's committee already beginning to bear good fruit.

Numerous other crowded meetings were held during the spring, which contributed largely to the formation of public opinion on the subject of fiscal reform. A reference to these enables us to trace the gradual change in the popular mind, from apathy to attention, from attention to inquiry, and from inquiry to conviction. It will thereby be seen how groundless and erroneous is the impression that still exists among some people, and especially among our foreign friends, that our adoption of the free-trade system was due, not to the slow growth and steady progress of reasoning and principle, but to sudden impulse, springing out of sudden calamity; and that our free-trade policy was the result, not of previous conviction, but of immediate necessity arising from the Irish famine of 1846. It will be abundantly clear that many years before that unforeseen and lament-

1811. able event, a large body of able, enlightened and earnest men, deeply imbued with the truth of free-trade principles, had made them popular by making them evident, and had thus roused in the minds of our leading statesmen a spirit of inquiry that ended in their conversion. We consider it of great importance that the truth should be known as to the origin of the free-trade movement. It will be seen that the abolition of most of our import duties had been effected, and the repeal of all duty on foreign corn had been demanded, and nearly conceded, before the potato failure in Ireland had occurred. How, therefore, can an antecedent effect be owing to a subsequent cause? It may by possibility be argued that Tenterden steeple is the cause of the Goodwin Sands; but by what process of reasoning could the Great Exhibition of 1851 be attributed to the Crimean War of 1854?

But even supposing that, by a reversal of the law of logical sequence, our free-trade tendencies, nearly matured as they were into actual practice by 1845, did originate in that Irish calamity which occurred the year after, what then? If free trade in that conjuncture was the sole remedy for our disasters, how does that prove that free trade is hurtful? If that system were really injurious, how came it that our resort to it did not intensify instead of healing our woes? If it was the only regimen that could restore us, at a calamitous period, to our political health and vigour, is that a plea for branding it as unhealthy and debilitating? No! Even supposing that we did adopt free trade as a desperate remedy for a desperate state of things, which is not the case, our speedy recovery and our subsequent unequalled progress in material prosperity would only tend to prove that the system is beneficially operative, both in removing the evils and promoting the welfare of nations.

CHAPTER IV.
(1841.)

The Whig Ministry propose a Fixed Duty of 8s. per quarter on Wheat, in lieu of the Sliding Scale—Their Budget—They are Defeated on the Sugar Duties—Dissolution of Parliament—New House of Commons—Richard Cobden—Sir Robt. Peel's Administration—State of the Country—Operations of the Anti-Corn-Law League.

PARLIAMENT was opened by the Queen, on the 26th January. On the 30th April, Lord John Russell announced that on the 30th May he should move "That the House resolve itself into a Committee of the whole House, to consider of the Acts relating to the trade in corn." This sudden and unexpected notification took the House by surprise and elicited vehement cheering from all sides. The unanimity of the cheers proceeded, however, from a variety of causes. The Conservative opposition cheered, because they saw in the announcement a confession of weakness; the Ministerialists, because they saw in it a hope of recovering popularity; the Free-traders, because they saw in it the first official concession to their demands. The wording of the notice was almost identical with that used over and over again by Mr. Villiers in those annual motions, which the Ministers had joined the Protectionists in opposing and negativing by large majorities year after year. A great and indubitably a sudden change of front! Had the opinions of Ministers undergone a change through the arguments propounded by the Anti-Corn-Law League, or was this merely an attempt on their part to prolong their tenure of office by making a bid for popular support? Not improbably a combination in various degrees of both influences swayed the members of the Ministry.

On the 7th of May, Lord John Russell defined the change which he intended to propose in the "Acts relating to the trade in corn." His measure would abolish the sliding-scale, and substitute for it a fixed duty of 8s. per quarter on wheat, 4s. 6d. on barley, and 3s. 4d. on oats. The formal motion to that effect was not to be made in Parliament till the end of the month, and this notice was given early, no doubt with a view to elicit some expression of the public voice in its favour. If that was the design, it signally failed. The measure attracted faint praise from a few, but the many received it with either condemnation or indifference. The Conservatives branded it as confiscation; while the Free-traders had repeatedly declared that they would be satisfied with nothing short of total repeal. Even from some of the moderate adherents to the Whig party, the proposition met with adverse criticism; it was an unequal tax on an article so widely fluctuating in price as corn, since 8s. per quarter was a tax of 10 per cent. on wheat at 80s. per quarter, and of 20 per cent. when the price was 40s. per quarter; it was an impossible tax under circumstances of not infrequent occurrence, since it was absurd to suppose that the people of England would submit to a tax of 8s. being levied, when the price of wheat was 70s. or 80s.; and it was a precarious source of revenue, since when English wheat was cheap and abundant, there would be neither importation nor revenue, while it was when bread was scarce and dear that the duty would yield the largest revenue; so that it would tax the people most heavily at the precise moment that they were least able to bear it.

Meanwhile, Ministers brought forward their financial Budget for 1841, and as the measures which it embodied were all decided steps in the direction of free-trade principles, it deserves some little attention. It exhibited a deficiency, to be made good, of more than £2,000,000. This deficit Ministers proposed to meet, not by the imposition of fresh taxes, but by the laudable expedient, novel at that time, of reducing those taxes which tended to lessen consumption, thus, at the same time, enriching the Treasury and adding to the comforts of the people. "I propose," said the Chancellor of the Exchequer (F. T. Baring), " to obtain the required supplies without adding to the burdens of the people. . . . The present duty on Colonial timber is 10s. a load, and on the Baltic timber 55s. This duty I propose to modify by raising that on Colonial to 20s., and reducing that on Baltic timber to 50s. a load. From this change I anticipate an increased revenue of £600,000. . . . I intend proposing to leave the duty on Colonial sugar at the present amount of 24s. per cwt., but that on foreign sugar, now amounting to 63s., I propose to reduce to 36s. per cwt. From this change I expect a further augmentation to the revenue of £700,000."

1841. He then went on to say that the balance of the deficiency he hoped to make good out of an increased revenue from foreign corn, resulting from the measure touching the Corn Laws that would shortly be brought forward.

This Budget caused a great sensation throughout the country. It was the first official recognition of the principle that private interests should give way to the public good. The Canadian timber merchants, the West Indian sugar-planters, the English landholders, were wild with indignation at this invasion of their monopolies. Their outcries, denunciations, and protests, were the exact types of those reproduced by the Protectionists of the present day all the world over. "The interests interfered with," they said, "were of considerable importance. They were very prosperous; why could not people leave them alone? Why should a parcel of restless, innovating busy-bodies, calling themselves scientific inquirers, come and disturb them? England was doing very well on the whole, and why worry things as they were by a morbid straining after things as they should be, or make the present uncomfortable in the doubtful hope of making the future happy? Besides, England must indubitably go to the dogs if the people spent their money on the produce of foreign labour instead of spending it on Canadian timber, or West Indian sugar, or English corn. What if the English people did pay dearer? The extra money went to support Colonial and native industry. Besides, it was give and take. If the timber, sugar, and landed interests were protected, so were all the rest; so were Tom the hardwareman, Dick the shipowner, and even Harry the cotton manufacturer. If each did take something from all the rest, it was made up by all the rest taking something from each. As to the working man, high prices were a blessing to him, as they procured for him higher money wages. Wages, when the quartern loaf was at eighteenpence, must of course be higher than when it was at sixpence," &c. &c.

Fortunately for England these reasonings made no impression whatever on the great mass of the British public; and, indeed, it is not improbable that their transparent sophistry hastened the conversion of some of the leading statesmen.

The object of the Conservative opposition was not so much to defeat the Budget as to oust the Ministers. As a battle-field, they chose the question of the Sugar duties, and Lord Sandon moved a resolution to the effect—"That considering the efforts and sacrifices which Parliament and the country have made for the abolition of the slave-trade and slavery . . . this House is not prepared . . . to adopt the measures proposed by Her Majesty's Government for the reduction of the duty on foreign sugars." A debate ensued, which lasted eight nights, and terminated on the 18th of May. It resulted in a defeat of the Ministers by thirty-six votes, there being 317 in favour of the resolution, and 281 against it. In Sir Robert Peel's able speech on this occasion, he objects to the change in the sugar duties as favourable to slavery, and to a fixed duty on corn as of doubtful permanency, but there are traces in it of a subdued tone in regard to a protectionist policy. For instance, in his perora-

1841. tion, he says :—"It is not the measures themselves which you introduce that are injurious, but they lose grace and favour in the public eye when it is believed that they do not spring from your deliberate will, are not formed in consequence of the conviction of your own minds, but are proposed merely for the purpose of propping up your fallen fortunes, and conciliating the favour of a particular party to whose support you look." He could hardly announce in clearer terms that his attack was directed more against the men themselves than against their measures.

It had been expected that Ministers, after so decisive a defeat, would at once have resigned. But they held on, and gave notice that they would bring forward their motion as to the Corn Laws on the 4th June. Sir Robert Peel was too able a parliamentary strategist to allow the Whigs to dissolve Parliament and appeal to the country on Anti-Corn-Law issues, and accordingly on the 27th May he moved a vote of want of confidence in Ministers. It was carried by 312 votes to 311, placing the Ministry in a minority of one. This left them no alternative but resignation or dissolution. They resorted to the latter. On the 22nd June, Parliament was prorogued, and the dissolution was proclaimed on the next day.

There could be no two opinions as to the part which the Anti-Corn-Law League, the recognised representative of the Free-trade party, should take in the forthcoming elections. They looked for few or no concessions from the Tories,—they looked for some but no important concessions from the Whigs,—and they therefore determined to trust only to themselves and to their own efforts. Crowded and enthusiastic meetings were held at Manchester, Liverpool, and many other places, at which the deputies detached for the purpose by the League, mostly headed by the indefatigable Richard Cobden, overcame all resistance and exercised supreme influence. In vain did the Chartists, playing, unwittingly or not, the game of the Tories, seek by every means in their power to disturb these meetings and divert them to their own purposes; they were out-talked, out-reasoned, and out-voted by overwhelming majorities. The popular voice responded energetically to the League's appeal, and the total abolition of all taxation on the people's food, whether fixed or sliding, became the unanimous cry in the manufacturing districts.

The elections resulted in a large majority for Sir R. Peel and his adherents. The reaction against the Whig Administration was decisive, but it did not excite much surprise. Their parliamentary majority had been continuously decreasing for some time past. The useful measures which they had passed, such as postal reform, and other similar improvements, were looked upon as small results, compared with what they might have achieved during so long a Ministerial reign, supported, as they were till recently, by a powerful majority. Their irresolute, faint-hearted action in the matter of the Corn Laws alienated from them some of their own party, while it totally failed to secure the adhesion of the Free-traders. The condition of the country was distressful, its finances embarrassed, and a resort to the great administrative and financial capacity of Sir Robert

1841. Peel was determined upon by the majority of the electors.

The new Parliament met on the 19th of August. The Queen's Speech was drawn up by the moribund Ministry in a tone that bespoke far livelier tendencies towards free trade than they had ever exhibited before, when they had the power to carry their theories into practice. It contained such passages as the following: "It will be for you to consider whether some of these duties (import duties on foreign goods) are not so trifling in amount as to be unproductive to the revenue, while they are vexatious to commerce. You may further examine whether the principle of protection, upon which others of these duties are founded, be not carried to an extent injurious alike to the income of the State and the interests of the people. Her Majesty is desirous that you should consider the laws which regulate the trade in corn. It will be for you to determine whether these laws do not aggravate the natural fluctuations of supply, . . and by their operation diminish the comfort and increase the privations of the great body of the community."

The amendment to the Address was proposed in the House of Lords by the Earl of Ripon, and carried against the Ministers by a majority of 72. A similar amendment was proposed in the House of Commons by Mr. Stuart Wortley, and, after four nights' debate, it was supported by 360 votes against 269, showing that in the newly-constituted House the majority against Ministers was 91, and that their tenure of power was at an end.

This debate was rendered memorable by its being the first in which Richard Cobden, the new member for Stockport, took part. This man—the son of a Sussex yeoman—a Clitheroe calico-printer who started in business on a borrowed capital of £500, and whose only instruments throughout his political career were pamphlets and speeches, has earned imperishable renown and made his name an object of affectionate reverence, not only among Englishmen but all the world over, by his masterly advocacy of the principles of "Free trade, peace, and good-will among nations." Great as were his abilities, he had a distrust of them approaching to humility; but such was his intense earnestness that, in the presence of a duty to be performed, his nervous timidity vanished. One of the most gentle and sympathetic of men, it was very distasteful to him to use harsh or bitter words, and yet, when the necessity arose, he forced his nature, and his denunciations of wrong or injustice were vehement and withering.

Of eloquence in the rhetorical sense, he had none; but he had complete mastery over the facts and arguments connected with his subject,—his language was at once lucid and concise,—his logic quick at detecting, and acute at demolishing, a sophism,—he abounded in apposite illustrations and anecdotes,—he went straight to the hearts of his hearers by home thrusts and direct appeals to their sense and feeling,—he was often familiar and colloquial, but never tedious, trite, or feeble, for he always grappled with his topic at close quarters, so that every word told and every sentence had a point. As to oratorical adornments or graces of

1841. elocution, he never aimed at them, but when thoroughly roused, either by irritating opposition or by the congenial sympathy of his audience, there would occasionally flash out of his speeches some sudden, bright inspiration, couched in a few glowing words, which would excite the more enthusiasm from its rareness and brevity. His delivery was, like his language, plain and homely, but it was as genial and impressive. It was that of a thoroughly sincere man, who intensely felt what he expressed, and whose words were the exact reflex of his inward thoughts. Often was he branded as an enthusiast and a visionary, but his bitterest opponent never taxed him with duplicity.

In his personal intercourse, he was gentle, sympathetic, and singularly unassuming. He unconsciously exercised over all who came into contact with him, whether relations, friends, or strangers, that undefinable magnetic influence which few possess, and which none, if they have it not, can acquire—an influence which irresistibly attracts attention and regard, sometimes deference and sympathy. He received everybody, from the highest to the lowest, with the same frank and simple courtesy, and his condolence and assistance were extended to every sufferer by wrong, whether national, sectional, or personal. To quote an able representative of the working classes: " A cause might be despised, obscure, or poor, he not only helped it all the same—he helped it all the more. . . . . In the day of triumph he shrank modestly on one side and stood in the common ranks; but in the dark or stormy days of unfriended truth he was always to the front."

He was thoroughly English in tastes, habits, and predilections, but, according to his creed, the interests of England were not only consistent, but identical, with those of mankind at large. He repudiated and abominated the doctrine that the prosperity of one country is incompatible with the prosperity of the rest. He was deeply convinced, and always spoke and acted on the conviction, that the precise contrary is the truth, and that each nation is most prosperous when all the rest are prosperous. As Sir Louis Mallet expresses it in his excellent introduction to "Cobden's Political Works": "Cobden believed that the real interests of the individual, of the nation, and of all nations, are identical." It is to this enlarged and cosmopolitan view of the relations between man and man, irrespective of the artificial boundaries mapped out between nation and nation, and also to the personal intercourse he held with the leading men of all countries during his frequent travels on the Continent, that Cobden owed the universality of his fame.

When, in the plenitude of his powers and at the zenith of his career, he was taken from our midst, a pang of regret throbbed throughout the whole of the civilised world. His loss was hardly more deplored, or his memory more eulogised, at home than it was abroad. Well did Drouyn de Lhuys, the French Foreign Minister, in his official despatch on the occasion, designate him "the international man." His influence was purely personal, for he held no office; but it was all the more weighty and wide-spread. He was indefatigable in using it, and he never used it

1841. except in a cause which he deemed just and holy. Plutarch's pen has drawn no nobler character.

On the 30th August, Her Majesty's Answer to the amended Address was delivered to the House of Commons. Its pith was contained in the following passage: "Ever anxious to listen to the advice of my Parliament, I will take immediate measures for the formation of a new Administration." The task was of course assigned to Sir Robert Peel, among whose colleagues the most noted were the Duke of Wellington, Lord Stanley, and Sir James Graham. From a Ministry so constituted, it seemed to most people vain to expect the adoption of a liberal commercial policy. But Sir Robert Peel had on various occasions intimated his willingness to amend the details of the existing Corn Laws, and had reserved to himself a certain independence of action with regard to his commercial policy. In his speech on the Address occur the following passages: "If you ask me whether I bind myself to the maintenance of the existing (corn) law in its details, or if you say that this is the condition on which the agricultural interest give me their support, I say that on that condition I will not accept their support. . . . If I accept office, it shall be by walking in the open light and in the direct paths of the Constitution. If I exercise power, it shall be upon my conception—perhaps imperfect, perhaps mistaken, but my sincere conception—of public duty. That power I will not hold unless I can hold it consistently with the maintenance of my own opinions." Noble words, on which his subsequent acts presented the best practical commentary.

On the other hand, even a Prime Minister is not omnipotent, and it would be very difficult for him to enforce concessions distasteful to the majority of the Cabinet. Moreover, Sir Robert Peel announced that it was not his intention to propose any definite measures of importance during the present session, and after some necessary routine work, Parliament was prorogued on the 8th of October.

Meanwhile, the state of the country was most deplorable. A bad harvest, the universal stagnation of trade, and a financial crisis had combined to spread the deepest distress and desolation among all classes of the people. But it was in the manufacturing districts that the sufferings were most frightful. Some of the details are quite appalling, and testify to an intensity and universality of destitution, starvation, and misery to which no period of temporary distress since the adoption of free trade in England can show the slightest approach. In Leeds, there were 20,936 persons whose average earnings were under one shilling a week. In Nottingham, 10,580 persons (nearly a fifth of the population) were in the receipt of parochial relief. In most of the leading trades of Birmingham, the men were earning one-half and, in some cases, one-third of their usual wages, while some of the masters were so near ruin that they had, on a Saturday night, to pawn their goods to pay their men's wages. In Paisley, thirty failures took place within two months, and one-third of the wage-receivers were thrown upon the public for support. In Manchester, 12,000 families, after having pawned every article of furniture and of dress with which they could

1841. possibly dispense, were supported by voluntary charitable contributions. One-third of the population of Coventry was out of work. "In Spitalfields, 8,000 looms were idle, and 24,000 persons thrown upon parochial relief. In the Metropolis, 1,000 letter-press compositors and 9,000 tailors were altogether without work."* But enough! There is no need to multiply instances to substantiate the fact. And while "protection to native industries" thus failed to find employment and wages for the native workman, it artificially raised upon him the price of the bread on which he lived; for the duty on foreign wheat was then, by the sliding scale, 24s. 8d. per quarter!

No wonder that a cry of indignation arose against the new Ministry for proroguing Parliament, and postponing measures of relief, until the ensuing year. And yet it was not altogether an unreasonable demand that Sir Robert Peel and his colleagues should be allowed some time to deliberate, to compare their views, and to concert their plan of operations. When taunted by Lord John Russell for the delay, the retort was effective: "If you think," replied Peel, "that commercial distress is attributable to the operation of the Corn Laws; if you think that these are at the root of the privation and suffering to which the labouring classes are exposed; what has been your neglect of duty in permitting those five years to elapse, during which you have held office, without bringing forward a proposition for the remedy of these abuses!"

The only effect of the Ministerial changes on the

* Dunckley's "Charter of Nations," p. 67.

operations of the Free-trade party, represented by the National Anti-Corn-Law League, was to stimulate them to increased activity. During the six months that elapsed between the formation of the new Ministry and the Session of 1842, the work was incessant. The leaders of the League made innumerable speeches at innumerable public meetings. The lecturers of the League addressed crowded audiences in as quick a succession as they could travel from place to place. The publications of the League were issued in millions, and found access to the smallest hamlet in the kingdom. We must cite a few of the most notable instances of the League's leverage on public opinion. A conference of ministers of religion of all denominations, from all parts, was convened at the Town Hall, Manchester, for the 17th of August. It was attended by 700 ministers, to all of whom, during their stay of one week, the hospitality of the various members of the League was respectively extended. The conference lasted four days; it was addressed by Richard Cobden, George Thompson, and others, contributed valuable information as to the condition and state of feeling prevailing in remote districts of the kingdom, and passed several resolutions in which the religious aspect of the question was forcibly urged. Over a large and influential section of the community these proceedings had a powerful effect.

On the 17th of November, 120 delegates met at Manchester from various parts of the kingdom. The principal feature in the plan of proceedings which they concerted was the copious and timely preparation of petitions, as embodied in the following resolution :

1841. "That all the present Anti-Corn-Law Associations . . . proceed immediately to get up petitions, and that it is very desirable that all petitions should be ready for presentation prior to the assembling of Parliament." It is to their business-like attention to such practical matters of detail that the League owed much of their success.

Nor were these gatherings in furtherance of an important political and social object confined to the sterner sex. The ladies of Lancashire took their part in the work, and occasionally held monster tea-meetings, at which they were addressed by some of the leaders of the movement, and most frequently by George Thompson, whose peculiarly impassioned language and thrilling accents secured him great favour from female audiences. It was at these meetings that the scheme originated of a bazaar to be held on a large scale in aid of the funds of the League, and a ladies' committee was appointed to report as to the means of carrying out the design. With the view of making the demonstration a national one, an appeal for contributions of articles for sale was made to all parts of the country, and it met with a most liberal response. Under the auspices of an active ladies' committee, of which Mrs. Cobden was chosen president, the bazaar was held early in 1842 at the Theatre Royal, Manchester, with signal success. It lasted ten days, and resulted in a net balance of about £9,000—an important addition to the funds of the League.

CHAPTER V.
(1842.)

Sir Robt. Peel's Modification of the Corn Law pleases no one—Mr. Villiers' Amendment for Entire Repeal Rejected—A Bold Budget—Income Tax imposed—Reduction of Import Duties on 750 Foreign Articles.

THE year 1842 opened under gloomy auspices. Universal distress was prevalent among the working classes—hence Chartist disaffection and disturbances—commerce was languishing, and the ranks of merchants and manufacturers had been decimated by failures—the national revenue had year by year been diminishing, while the national expenditure was increasing, and there was a heavy deficit to make good—there had arisen a loud cry and a formidable agitation for a free commercial policy, and specially for a total repeal of all duties on corn—and to meet these troubles there was a new Parliament led by a new Ministry, from whom it was rather measures of repression than measures of relief that might be expected. No wonder that the people looked with more anxiety than hope to Sir Robert Peel's undisclosed policy, and awaited its announcement with impatient curiosity.

Such were the circumstances under which the Session of 1842 was opened by the Queen in person on the 3rd February. The following two passages in the Queen's Speech attracted marked attention:—" I recommend to your consideration the state of the laws which affect the importation of corn and other articles, the produce of foreign countries. . . . I have observed with deep regret the continued distress in

1842. the manufacturing districts of the country. The sufferings and privations which have resulted from it have been borne with exemplary patience and fortitude." The latter sentence expressed becoming sympathy with the sufferings of the people: the former expressed the intention of affording them some degree of relief. In the debate on the Address, no information was given as to the nature of the contemplated fiscal changes, but Sir Robert Peel gave notice that on the 9th he should move that the House resolve itself into a Committee of the whole House, to take into consideration the laws which affect the importation of corn.

During the intervening week of suspense, the public mind was painfully agitated. The only circumstance that afforded any clue to conjecture was the resignation of the Duke of Buckingham, which had taken place a few days before. In the debate on the Address, the Duke had thus accounted for his withdrawal from the Ministry: "During his connection with the present Government," he said, "a measure was proposed for an alteration in the Corn Laws, which he found it impossible to support." Hence it was clear that a modification of those obnoxious laws was to be proposed, but as to the extent or direction of the change great differences of opinion existed.

The Anti-Corn-Law League, however, determined that there should be no ambiguity as to their views. The delegates met in London, at the Crown and Anchor Tavern, on the 8th, and all of them, 600 in number, enthusiastically concurred in the determination to be satisfied with nothing short of the total abrogation of all duties on the admission of foreign corn. The chairman, John Brooks, announced that on the previous day an interview had been sought with Sir Robert Peel, which had been declined on the plea of "pre-engagement." On the 9th, the day fixed for Sir Robert Peel's announcement, the delegates met in full numbers, and after some animated speeches a sudden and unpremeditated proposition was made by a Mr. Boultbee, of Birmingham, that the deputies should proceed in a body to the House of Commons. It was carried by acclamation, and 500 members, many of them ministers of religion, proceeded two and two, arm-in-arm, along the Strand and down Parliament Street to the House. They sought admission to the lobby of the House: this was refused. They stood, however, on the pavement opposite, and saluted the different members as they passed with cries of "No sliding scale," "Total repeal," &c. After a little time, under the pressure of the police, the deputies withdrew, and with three ringing cheers for the "Repeal of the Corn Laws," they proceeded up Parliament Street. "Just at Privy Gardens they met Sir Robert Peel proceeding in his carriage to the House. He seemed to think at first that they were going to cheer him, but when he heard the angry shouts of 'No Corn Law,' 'Down with monopoly,' 'Give bread and labour,' he leaned back in his carriage, grave and pale."*

The House was crowded with members, and the galleries were full to overflowing. Messengers were

* Archibald Prentice, "History of the Anti-Corn-Law League," Vol. I., page 310.

1842. in attendance outside to convey in the quickest way to all parts of the country, and to all countries, the substance of the Minister's communication. Sir Robert Peel was heard with breathless attention. "A listening senate hung upon his lips." His speech was an elaborate one, though hardly equal to many other of his oratorical efforts. The scheme which he brought forward was simply a modified sliding scale. The following is a summary of it as given by himself: "When corn (wheat) is at 59s. per quarter and under 60s. the duty at present is 27s. 8d.; when it is between those prices, the duty I propose is 13s. When the price of corn is at 50s., the existing duty is 36s. 8d., increasing as the price falls; instead of which I propose when corn is at 50s. that the duty shall only be 20s., and that that duty shall in no case be exceeded. At 56s. the existing duty is 30s. 8d.; the duty I propose at that price is 16s. At 60s. the existing duty is 26s. 8d.; the duty I propose at that price is 12s. At 63s. the existing duty is 23s. 8d.; the duty I propose is 9s. At 64s. the existing duty is 22s. 8d.; the duty I propose is 8s. At 70s. the existing duty is 10s. 8d.; the duty I propose is 5s. Therefore it is impossible to deny, on comparing the duty I propose with that which exists at present, that it will cause a very considerable decrease of the protection which the present duty affords to the home grower."

Very little discussion ensued on that evening, members preferring to give some consideration to the proposal, and to reserve themselves for the regular debate which would come on in a few days. As soon as the details of Sir Robert Peel's measure became known, meetings were held in all the chief towns throughout the kingdom, at which the Government proposal was utterly condemned, and "total repeal" vehemently insisted upon. The land-owners would doubtless have preferred no change from the old system, but they sullenly accepted the change proposed, as being practically only a small disturbance of their monopoly.

The consumers of corn, however, saw very clearly that the concession so ostentatiously proffered by Sir Robert Peel was really none at all; and that they were called upon to recognise and accept a mere shadow as a substantial boon. The substitution of 20s. import duty instead of 36s. 8d. when wheat was at 50s. sounded well to the ear and looked well to the eye, but lost all value when submitted to analysis. A 20s. duty was just as prohibitory as one of 36s. 8d. Whether Sir Robert Peel lowered the duty to 20s. or raised it to 50s. did not make any real difference. At neither rate could foreign wheat come in. As somebody expressed it, a man may be drowned in 10 feet of water just as much as in 20 feet; and it would have been none the worse for him if the depth had been 50 feet. The same reasons which induced the landed interest to assent to the Ministerial measures, prompted the Free-traders to offer to them their most strenuous and uncompromising opposition.

The adjourned debate took place on the 14th February. Lord John Russell moved as an amendment:—"That this House, considering the evils which have been caused by the present Corn Laws, and especially by the fluctuations of the graduated or sliding scale, is not prepared to adopt the measure of Her Majesty's Government, which is founded on the same principles, and is likely to be attended by similar results." His speech was a very able one, and his motion was warmly supported by several members, among whom Mr. Roebuck and Lord Palmerston were conspicuous.

After four nights' debate, Lord John Russell's amendment was rejected by a majority of 123. Nothing daunted, Mr. Villiers brought forward, on the following Friday, his amendment for the entire abolition of all duties on corn. This elicited another interesting debate, which extended over five nights and gave rise to several effective speeches. None was more telling than that of Mr. Macaulay (afterwards Lord Macaulay). In answer to the argument that England ought "only casually" to be dependent on other countries for food supply, he said that "he preferred constant to casual dependence, for constant dependence became mutual dependence. . . . As to war interrupting our supplies, a striking instance of the fallacy of that assumption was furnished in 1810, during the height of the Continental System, when all Europe was against us, directed by a chief who sought to destroy us through our trade and commerce. In that year (1810) there were 1,600,000 quarters of corn imported, one-half of which came from France itself." His views as to Sir Robert Peel's proposed measure he thus summed up: —"It is a measure which settles nothing; it is a measure which pleases nobody; it is a measure which nobody asks for, and which nobody thanks him for;

it is a measure which will neither extend trade nor relieve distress."

Richard Cobden advocated Mr. Villiers' amendment with a vigour and vehemence which, while provoking the wrath, commanded the attention of his opponents. They might impugn his statements, and scoff at his inferences, but none could ignore the raciness and terse lucidity of his style. His address excited uproarious dissent, but it established his reputation as a Parliamentary debater, and secured to him for ever the ear of the House. A few extracts may afford some faint reflex of the compact directness and energy of his language. "I have heard it proposed," he said, "by a Prime Minister to fix the price of corn! . . . What an avocation for a Legislature! To fix a price on corn! Why, that should be done in the open markets by the dealers. You don't fix the price of cotton, or silk, or iron, or tin. . . . It appears that there are to be found gentlemen still at large who advocate the principle of the interposition of Parliament to fix the price at which articles should be sold. . . . I ask the right honourable baronet, and I pause for a reply—Is he prepared to carry out that principle in the articles of cotton and wool? (Hear, hear.)" Sir Robert Peel said it was impossible to fix the price of food by legislation. (Loud cheers from the Ministerial side.) Mr. Cobden: "Then on what are we legislating? (Great cheering from the Opposition.) . . . I ask the right honourable baronet whether, while he fixes his sliding-scale of prices so as to secure to the landowners 56s. per quarter for wheat, he has a sliding-scale for wages? . . . Let us

1842. only legislate, if you so please, for the introduction of corn when it is wanted. Exclude it as much as possible when it is not wanted. But what I supplicate for, on the part of the starving people, is that they, and not you, shall be the judge of when corn is wanted. By what right do you pretend to gauge the appetites and admeasure the wants of millions of people? . . . Are you prepared to deal even-handed justice to the people? If not, your law will not stand —nay, your House itself, if based upon injustice, will not stand."

Mr. Villiers' amendment was rejected by 393 votes against 90—a majority of 303.

Of the other stages of Sir Robert Peel's sliding-scale measure little need be said. A few additional amendments were moved both in the Commons and in the House of Lords, some by the Free-traders, some by the extreme Protectionists; but all met with the same fate, and were rejected by large majorities. A motion by Lord Brougham in the House of Lords for the total repeal of duties on corn was only supported by five peers. On the 29th of April the new Bill became law.

Meanwhile, on the 11th of March, Sir Robert Peel laid before the House his bold, broad, comprehensive, financial scheme in a speech of considerable length, which, for mastery of detail, clearness of exposition, and earnestness of appeal, has rarely been equalled. His plan was as simple as it was spirited. Its two main features were the imposition of an income-tax, and a revision of the tariff—the adoption of direct and a reduction of indirect taxation. He had to meet a deficiency of no less than £2,500,000. How was he to make it good? "The previous Government had laid an additional per-centage of 5 per cent. on the Customs and Excise, which, last year, instead of producing £5 on each £100, had only produced about 10s. . . . The country had therefore arrived at the limits of taxation on articles of consumption. . . . Should he revive old taxes, and go back to the Post-Office? At present the Post-Office produced no revenue at all, but rather occasioned a charge, but he did not think the recent reduction had yet had a sufficient trial to justify an increase upon postage. . . . He would propose, for a period of three years, an income-tax of 7d. in the £ (about 3 per cent.), from which he would exempt all incomes under £150. From this source he expected to raise £3,771,000. . . . On the other hand, he proposed to relax the commercial tariff. . . . Out of 1,200 articles paying duty, he recommended an abatement of duty on 750, leaving 450 untouched. In the special case of timber, he would lower the duty on foreign to 25s. a load, and let in the timber of Canada at a duty of 1s."

Those were the main topics of Sir Robert Peel's speech, which was listened to with profound attention. With the exception of a few slight changes in the silk duties introduced by Mr. Huskisson in 1823, the English tariff had till now remained in the same old barbarous state. It imposed duties on every conceivable article, raw or manufactured, that could be sent us from abroad. These duties were sometimes fixed, sometimes *ad valorem*, sometimes both on the same article. Many of them were differential, being

1842. higher on the produce of some countries and lower on that of others. They varied in their rates in the most capricious and unaccountable manner, as though they had been fixed at random or hit upon by lot. They were levied with the same ponderous and costly machinery, whatever might be the amount they yielded to the revenue, whether on the few tons annually imported of cochineal, or on the hundreds of cargoes of cotton and sugar. The official forms through which the collection of those duties permeated were most complex, and bristled with difficulties in the shape of conflicting valuations, differential rates, identification of nationalities, &c., &c., which necessitated abundance of oaths, declarations and affidavits, and of consequent perjury, and afforded irresistible temptations to bribery, to cheating, and finally to smuggling with all its attendant demoralising influences.

The aim of the Free-Trade party, represented by the Anti-Corn-Law League, was the removal of all these import duties, of which the duty on foreign corn was but one. This latter they selected as the special object of their attacks, not because it presented any peculiarity of principle, but because it was the most extensively injurious, the most generally obnoxious, and, at the same time, the most powerfully defended of all protected interests. That duty once abolished, the rest would be easy. Sir Robert Peel's tariff reform, incomplete and tentative as it was, was the first step (and the first is always the most important step) in the right direction. It was evident that Joseph Hume's Import Duties Committee, referred to at page 33, was beginning to bear fruit. The first breach in the fortress of Protection was made, and its fall would henceforward be only a matter of time.

The Whig party persistently opposed the imposition of an income-tax. They argued that it was unnecessary, and that the adoption of the budget which they had proposed on the eve of their resignation of power would be sufficient to place the finances of the country on a sound basis, without resorting to so extreme and unpopular a measure as an income tax, and they succeeded in obtaining a postponement to the 4th April of the further discussion on the subject. They no doubt expected that during the intervening period public opinion would declare itself loudly and unequivocally in condemnation of that inquisitorial tax, and that their hands would be strengthened by the popular outcry. If so, they were mistaken. The country was mute and acquiescent. The only agitation that prevailed was that against the Corn Laws, and was directed as much against Lord John Russell's 8s. duty as against Sir Robert Peel's sliding scale.

When the House re-assembled after the Easter recess, the question of the income tax was resumed. On the 8th of April Lord John Russell proposed an adverse amendment, which was rejected by 308 votes against 202. On the 18th of April Lord John came to the charge again, and moved that the Bill be read a first time that day six months. Again the Ministers triumphed, by a majority of 285 to 188.

In Committee various amendments were put forward. Mr. Roebuck proposed that 3½d. instead of 7d. be charged on incomes derived from professions, trades, and employments, and supported his views by

1842. powerful arguments. Mr. F. T. Baring proposed to exempt annuities, dividends, or shares held by foreigners not resident in Great Britain. But Ministers opposed every alteration to their measure; and when the House divided on the third reading, there appeared for the motion 199, against it 69, and it thus passed with a majority of 130. In the House of Lords it passed on the 21st of June by a majority of 71.

CHAPTER VI.

(1842.)

First Instalment of Tariff Reform—Chartism—Its Leaders advise a general "Strike"—Its Collapse—The Anti-Corn-Law League raises £50,000.

Sir Robert Peel's next task was, on the 5th of May, to introduce his limited but substantial measure of Free Trade, by the reduction of import duties on 750 articles of foreign produce. His able introductory speech was an admirable example of a subject abounding in dry details being treated by a master mind in such a manner as to excite interest and even create amusement. That his object distinctly was, in conformity with the principles of Free Trade, to suppress the monopolies of native producers, and secure cheapness to native consumers, is most clearly set forth in his speech. "We have attempted," he said, "to remove all absolute prohibitions upon the import on foreign articles, and to reduce duties which are so high as to be prohibitory, to such a scale as may admit of a fair competition with domestic produce. . . . . I contend that if there be any truth in the principles of either trade or arithmetic, the inevitable result must be to make a considerable reduction in the present price of living in this country as compared with the price of living in other countries." He diverted the House by reading a letter addressed to him by a person connected with the herring fishery, cautioning him not to lower the duty on foreign herrings, or else the Norwegian fishermen would undersell them (the Scotch), the writer adding with delicious simplicity, that he was "a thorough Free Trader in every other respect but herrings." He also read extracts from a letter or circular from a noted smuggler to a London firm, stating the premiums he charged for conveying French lace, veils, gloves, &c., *by the indirect channel*. The premiums varied from 8 to 13 per cent., and were, of course, " considerably below your Custom House duties."

He proceeded, by much ingenuity of explanation, to allay the apprehensions which his reduction in the duties on cattle and provisions had created in the minds of his agricultural supporters, and wound up by declaring his adhesion to the principles of Free Trade, to be carried out prudently, " with as small an amount of individual suffering as was compatible with regard for the public good." "I believe," he said, "that on the general principle of Free Trade there is now no great difference of opinion, and that all agree in the general rule that we should purchase in the cheapest market and sell in the dearest. . . . The example of England would ensure the general application of just principles with benefit to herself and to those who were wise enough to follow."

1542. In Committee the proposed tariff reform met with strenuous but unavailing opposition. The Whigs objected not to the principle, but to the details. Many of the old-fashioned Tories objected to both. Mr. R. Palmer declared that "he felt alarm because he did not know to what lengths the Government might not be led after they had begun legislating on Free-Trade principles;" adding, with instinctive prescience, "when the tariff was passed, the next step to be expected would be the repeal of the Corn Laws."

On the 23rd May the recalcitrant agriculturists broke out into open revolt. Mr. Miles, after stating that "a deputation of county and agricultural members had waited on Sir Robert Peel to endeavour to induce him to alter the duty on foreign cattle, but without success," proposed, by way of amendment, that "all live stock imported from foreign countries should be charged by weight." Both the Ministers, represented by Mr. Gladstone, and the Opposition, represented by Lord John Russell, united their forces against the amendment, and it was rejected by a majority of 267. In the House of Lords the opposition was even feebler, and the third reading was carried there by 52 votes against 9.

While the three great measures introduced by Government—the modified Corn Law, the Income Tax, and the Tariff Reform—were in the process of receiving the sanction of the Legislature the condition of the country had undergone no improvement. The distress was deep and universal. From the agricultural as well as from the manufacturing districts, from all the great centres of trade—Manchester, Birmingham, Glasgow, and Leeds—there came forth one great cry of agony. Merchants and manufacturers in great numbers succumbed to the pressure, and were driven into bankruptcy. Hundreds of thousands of industrious men were thrown out of employment, and subsisted either by private charity or out of the Poor's-rates, which had swollen into oppressive dimensions.

No wonder that among these hordes of starving and desperate men the Chartist leaders should have found willing hearers and numerous proselytes. The extent of their influence among the working classes may be measured by the following fact. On the 2nd of May, while the House was in committee on the Income Tax Bill, a petition of abnormal and portentous dimensions was brought into the lobby. Its prayer was "that the House of Commons do immediately, without alteration, deduction, or addition, pass into law the document entitled 'The People's Charter.'" It was said to bear no less than three millions of signatures. It was borne on the shoulders of sixteen men, who were escorted by a long and numerous procession. The folding-doors of the House were not sufficiently capacious to admit this "monster" petition. It had to be unrolled to get it into the House, where, being spread on the floor, its folds rose above the level of the table. It was presented by Mr. T. Duncombe, wondered at, spoken about, and soon forgotten.

But all the efforts of the Chartists to chafe discontent into riot, and to enlist physical force in their cause proved abortive. With rare exceptions the people remained patient and law-abiding. To this

1842. result the action of the Anti-Corn-Law League powerfully conduced. It led the people to aim at legitimate and attainable objects, instead of visionary schemes of organic changes in the Constitution, and taught them how to pursue those objects by lawful and peaceable methods.

On the 4th July the deputies from the various associations constituting the Anti-Corn-Law League met in London. After several conferences, at which accumulated evidence was obtained of the deplorable state of the country, it was determined to wait upon Sir Robt. Peel, and lay it before him. Accordingly, on the 25th, about 150 delegates proceeded in a body, at 11 o'clock by appointment, to Downing Street, where they were introduced to Sir Robt. Peel by Mr. P. A. Taylor. Several forcible statements were made by gentlemen who represented Liverpool, Manchester, the Staffordshire Potteries, Sheffield, Stockport, Bury, Leeds, and Forfar, to which the Minister listened with attention, but nothing was elicited from him except the stereotyped reply that he would lay the statements before Her Majesty's Government. He merely added, "I have nothing farther to communicate, unless it is to express my deep sympathy in the distresses of the country, and to thank you for the testimony you have borne, which I fear is incontestable." Almost all the Ministers were waited on by similar deputations, which enlarged upon the pressing necessity there was for Government to do "something" for the suffering people before Parliament was prorogued.

But these conferences led to no result. The Ministers were not prepared to resort to any supplementary measures to meet what they considered a transitory crisis. A motion made in parliament by Mr. Wallace to the effect of postponing the prorogation, was rejected by a large majority.

A last effort was made on the 21st July, when Mr. T. Duncombe moved an address to the Queen, praying that, if no improvement in the condition of the people took place after the prorogation, Parliament should be re-assembled to consider the question of an alteration in the commerce in corn. The Ministers, fatigued and irritated by so much persistency, opposed to it a mere passive resistance, abstained from speaking, and prepared to crush it by votes. But, taunted with this silence, and piqued into speech, Sir R. Peel burst into a scathing denunciation of such obstruction to public business. In a reply no less fierce and vehement, Richard Cobden retorted that the salvation of the people from famine or the workhouse was the essence of public business; and wound up by asking, "Would the right honourable baronet resist the appeals which had been made to him, or would he rather cherish the true interests of the country, and not allow himself to be dragged down by a section of the aristocracy? He must take sides, and that instantly; and should he, by so doing, displease his political supporters, there was an answer ready. He might say that he found the country in distress, and he gave it prosperity; that he found the people starving, and he gave them food; that he found the large capitalists of the country paralysed, and he made them prosperous." But Cobden and his party, though strong in the country, were weak in the House, and 156 votes against 64 affirmed the Ministerial policy.

1842.	The prorogation of Parliament took place on the 12th August by the Queen in person, and in her speech reference was made to "the prospects of a harvest more abundant than those of recent years," and also to "that depression which has affected many branches of manufacturing industry, and has exposed large classes of my people to privations and sufferings." But "privations and sufferings" do not come to an end through gracious and sympathetic references to them in a Queen's speech. Their extinction demanded some immediate and direct measures. None such were adopted. Ministers were content to wait for the gradual and indirect effect of that fiscal reform of which they had granted a limited instalment.

Meantime, during that unhappy autumn, the Chartist leaders did their utmost to ingraft popular disaffection on to popular distress. They adopted as desperate a line of policy as could possibly be conceived. Emissaries and lecturers were sent to all the great centres of manufacturing industry, to urge the half-employed workmen to join, on one and the same day, throughout the country, in one grand, universal strike.

The substance of their appeal to the men was this :—" Unless universal suffrage, and the other five points of the Charter, are passed into law, there can be no relief to your distress. Cheap bread and increased wages through Free Trade are mere lies, delusions, and shams to lure you away from insisting on your only remedy—universal suffrage. Your masters oppose it because they want to keep you in abject slavery. Compel its adoption! You are thousands to units. If you hesitate to use brute force, use at least the legal weapons placed in your hands. All that is produced is the produce of your work. Abstain from producing until universal suffrage becomes the law of the land, and your tyrants will at once be at your mercy. They will submit to anything sooner than close their mills, their foundries, their factories, and their shops. They are powerless against you if you are firm and unanimous. Give them the alternative of either adopting the Charter or incurring disorganisation, ruin, and bankruptcy, and the Charter will triumph, and speedily become the law of the land. Then, and not till then, will every one of you get a fair day's wage for a fair day's work. Spurn and scout the cant of the Anti-Corn-Law hypocrites. Their object is to prolong your serfdom, and beckon you away from your allegiance to the Charter. Show the power of numbers. The few domineer because the many know not their strength. Let every hand, at every factory, in every district, stop work on one and the same day, not to resume it until the Charter becomes the law of the land. Let one universal cry resound through the country—'No Charter, no work!'"

These ravings did not fall unheeded on the ears of destitute and ignorant men. Two or three days per week employment at scanty wages afforded so bare a pittance, that it seemed a small sacrifice to throw it up, on the chance of securing the Charter and the general abundance which it was guaranteed to ensure. The scheme was carried out extensively in many parts of the manufacturing districts, and the month of August was spent in struggles which ended in the discomfiture of the men, and only served to increase their distress and sufferings.

In Lancashire the number of those who, either from choice or on compulsion, took part in the proceedings was very considerable. To quote an eye-witness* :—"The movement, originating in Ashton-under-Lyne, Dukinfield, and Stalybridge, was almost without violence and simultaneous. All the hands in all the mills—23,000 in number—turned out at once on the morning of Monday, August the 8th, and deputies from their body induced 9,150 in Hyde and its neighbourhood to follow the example. Oldham was visited in the afternoon by numerous turn-outs from Ashton, who succeeded in causing the operatives to leave most of the mills. On Tuesday a body of several thousands proceeded from Ashton to Manchester. . . . Their demand at various mills that the hands should turn out was instantly complied with, the masters generally giving their hands full liberty to do as they pleased. . . No attempt at the destruction of machinery was made." Some meetings of the men were held, at which that crazy demagogue, Feargus O'Connor, was to have appeared, but he kept away. A few trifling collisions took place with the authorities; but, on the whole, the conduct of the multitude showed that the great majority consisted of honest and law-abiding men.

The masters met the movement in a judicious manner by assuming a quiet and passive attitude. The united body adopted and published the following resolution :—"That the mills and other public works

* Archibald Prentice. "History of the Anti-Corn-Law League."

of Manchester and Salford be not opened for work until the workpeople therein employed signify their desire to resume work." This calm, unresisting acquiescence in the cessation from work took the men by surprise, and greatly disheartened them. They had been assured that the masters would be at once driven into joining the cry for the Charter, whereas they quietly folded their arms and looked coolly on.

At this juncture Mr. John Bright of Rochdale, whom the working people well knew to be their staunch friend, issued an address, which, in a friendly spirit, but in forcible words, laid the truth before them. This eloquent and sympathetic appeal to the common sense of the men produced a powerful effect on them.

Similar scenes, but with rather more riot and lawlessness than in Lancashire, took place in other manufacturing and mining districts, and chiefly in Yorkshire (Leeds, Halifax, &c.), in Staffordshire (at the potteries and among the Dudley miners), in Wales at the chief collieries, and in Scotland among the Glasgow operatives. But in all these places delusive hopes soon vanished before stern realities. No work meant no wages; no wages meant no food. By the end of August all the turn-outs who could find work resumed it, the relations between wage-payers and wage-receivers were restored to their old footing, and the Chartist hallucination faded away. This outbreak had lasted three weeks. Within that short period, poverty, driven to despair, had listened to desperate counsels, tested them, found them wanting, and had renewed its allegiance to the dictates of common sense.

The Protectionist party loudly accused the Anti-

1842. Corn-Law League of having fomented these disturbances. They were, it was contended, the outcome of the cry for cheap food, and when reminded that the leaders of the League were the very masters against whom those disturbances were directed, they merely rejoined, with logical incoherency, "Then serve them right!" "Far from being the instigators, we were the sufferers!" cried the manufacturers. "Well," answered their opponents, "if you did not instigate this time, you did at some other; any how, it is quite right that you should be the sufferers." A good specimen of party polemics.

The exertions of the Anti-Corn-Law League from August to December, 1842, were incessant, and richly deserved the success which they achieved. Innumerable public meetings fully reported, the distribution of "bales" of tracts, the delivery of lectures wherever there was an audience to listen, the dissemination of Free-Trade principles in every form, in every place, and by every conceivable means except force—and, to clench all, the determination (which was carried out) to raise a fund of £50,000 for the purpose of "educating" the country — abundantly testified to the vigour and energy of the League.

In relation to the fund to be raised, the first intimation of it was given by Richard Cobden in a speech which he delivered at a meeting of the League on the 6th October, George Wilson being, as usual, in the chair. In the course of it he said : "Money is wanted to carry on this conflict as it should be carried on for the next six months. Our friend in the chair has a project (you will be startled when I tell you of it) by which he intends to subsidise the country to the extent of £50,000. Well, that is just a million shillings; we had two millions of petitioners for the repeal of the Corn Laws; where is the difficulty of getting a million shillings?" In a subsequent speech he said: "The monopolist papers say that we shall not be able to raise the £50,000 fund. Why, the fact is, the Council begin to feel that the money raised will exceed that sum. You see what a capital estimate they had formed of the spirit abroad. They had not waited for the country to respond; they said, 'We'll spend the money first; we'll put ourselves in pledge for it, and we'll trust to our bread-eating countrymen to take us out of pawn.'" The money was raised.

CHAPTER VII.

(1843.)

State of the Country—Scene between Sir R. Peel and Mr. Cobden—Activity of the Anti-Corn-Law League—Debate on Mr. Villiers' Annual Motion.

THE year 1843 opened in gloom and despondency. Trade prospects had not yet improved among the commercial and manufacturing classes, although a bountiful harvest had mitigated their privations by making wheat cheaper. On the other hand, the farmers were heavy losers by the fall in the value of wheat, because they were paying rents based on starvation prices. Let us review the current prices of wheat for six years as given by Sir Robert Peel in his

1843. speech on Lord Howick's motion: "On the 2nd January, 1836, wheat was 59s. the quarter; on the same day in 1838 it was 52s. 4d.; in 1839 it was 78s. 2d.; in 1840, 56s. 5d.; in 1841, 61s.; in 1842, 63s. 1d.; and in 1843, 46s. 11d." These fluctuations, which it was the avowed and special function of that ingenious and complicated instrument, the sliding scale, to prevent and avert, are startling. The rise between 1838 and 1839 was 25s. 10d. per quarter; the fall between 1842 and 1843 was 16s. 2d. per quarter. The former ruined the traders, the latter ruined the farmers; the landholders being enriched in both cases at the expense of now one, and now the other class.

The diminished spending power of the impoverished community was clearly manifested by a falling off, the last quarter of 1842, in the two important branches of Excise and Customs, of no less than £1,300,000—a falling off equivalent to £5,000,000 per annum.

It was under these circumstances that the Session was opened on the 2nd February. The debate on the Address was remarkable only for a declaration of Sir Robert Peel which deeply disappointed the advocates of progress. "I did last Session make," he said, "more extensive changes in the commerce of this country than were made at any former period . . . . but I did not lead the House to suppose that I would go on, year after year, introducing extensive changes." He concluded by avowing that, "Her Majesty's Government have not in contemplation any amendment of the Corn Laws."

This policy of inaction incited the Opposition to an attack. On the 18th February Lord Howick moved for a Committee of the whole House to investigate the causes of the distress. An interesting debate ensued, which continued for five nights. The mover's speech contained a luminous exposition of Free-Trade principles, to which Mr. Gladstone, in his reply, expressed his ready adhesion, but argued for the necessity of proceeding cautiously in their practical adoption. "Lord Howick," he said, "might have spared himself the trouble of advancing abstract principles when the real question was one of time and degree." Sir James Graham, in his speech against the motion, was still more outspoken as to the needlessness of discussing Free-Trade principles in the House. "By most men," he said, "these principles were now acknowledged to be the principles of common sense, and the outlines of these principles were now disputed but by few. The time had long gone by when this country could exist solely as an agricultural country. We were now a commercial people."

On the fifth evening of the debate an exciting scene took place in which Peel and Cobden, two of the most prominent men in this our history, were the chief actors. For its better comprehension, it will be necessary to state that a few days before, on the 21st January, Mr. Drummond, the private secretary and intimate friend of Sir Robert Peel, had been fired at in the street and mortally wounded by a man who was afterwards proved to have been insane. There appeared every reason to believe that the assassin had mistaken Mr. Drummond for Sir Robert Peel, and had intended to murder the Prime Minister. The effect of this melancholy event which was to him at once a personal

1843. bereavement and a personal menace, on Sir Robert Peel's nervous system was visible in the unusual irritability of manner which he about this time displayed. On the evening in question he yielded to the excitement of the moment, and was seduced into a regrettable indiscretion.

Mr. Cobden, at the close of a very forcible speech, said: "Sir Robert Peel had it in his power to carry the measures necessary for the people; and if he had not that power as a Minister, he would have it by resigning his office. Sir Robert Peel should be held individually responsible: the electoral body would force him to do them justice." Whereupon the Prime Minister rose, and, with great vehemence of manner, exclaimed: "Sir, the honourable gentleman has stated here very emphatically, what he has more than once stated at the Conference of the Anti-Corn-Law League, that he holds me individually" (these last words were pronounced with great solemnity of manner and elicited emphatic and prolonged cheering from the Ministerial benches, during which the House presented an appearance of extreme excitement)—"individually responsible for the distress and suffering of the country; that he holds me personally responsible (renewed cheering). Be the consequences of those insinuations what they may (vehement cheering)—never will I be influenced by menaces (continued cheering)—to adopt a course which I consider—(the rest of the sentence was lost in renewed shouts from the Ministerial benches).

Mr. Cobden rose, and said: "I did not say that I held the right hon. gentleman personally responsible.

(Shouts from the Ministerial benches of 'yes, yes; you did, you did'; mingled with cries of 'order' and 'chair.') I have said that I held the right honourable gentleman responsible by virtue of his office (shouts of 'no, no' and confusion), as the whole context of what I said was sufficient to explain (renewed cries of 'no, no' from the Ministerial benches). By degrees the commotion arising out of this incident subsided, and Sir Robert Peel himself soon recovered his equilibrium, for he made a very eloquent speech, and the motion was lost by 306 votes against 191. At the close of the debate, Mr. Cobden again rose to disavow the meaning which had been imputed to him in the employment of the word "individually"; and Sir Robert Peel in a somewhat cold and distant manner accepted the explanation.

The impression throughout the country was that the interpretation put on Richard Cobden's words was unjustifiable and absurd. No one who knew anything of him and his career, or of the Anti-Corn-Law League and its leaders, could imagine how the most distant idea of their instigating or countenancing assassination could have entered into the heads of sane men. The only excuse for it, or rather the only mode of accounting for it, is nervous excitement and sudden impulse in the feverish heat of debate. Sir Robert Peel afterwards freely confessed his error, and made noble amends for it.

The imputation on Richard Cobden far from tarnishing his fame, largely extended his influence and popularity. Numerous meetings were held throughout the country for the special purpose of expressing their

1843. indignation at the charge, their thanks for his exertions, their confidence in his character, and their admiration for his talents. Of all these meetings, it will be sufficient to describe one. It took place at the newly-built Free Trade Hall, at Manchester. Under the span of that noble roof, which, within the area of one room, contained nearly as much cubic space as Westminster Hall itself, nine thousand persons assembled to bear testimony on the occasion.

The able and energetic chairman of the League, George Wilson, presided, and roused the feelings of the audience to the utmost by his vigorous repudiation of the charge against Mr. Cobden and his colleagues. He summed up thus: "In the name of all who are included in this accusation, I deny all alliance with, and approbation or knowledge of, any agent or means, other than those that are peaceful and moral, for the accomplishment of our object. (Great cheering.) In the name of the ladies—(great cheering)—the occupants of those galleries—(immense cheering, the whole of the vast assemblage in the body of the hall waving their hats)—who have graced our meetings on many a previous occasion, and who are included in that base attack—I deny it! (Deafening cheers.) In the name of the thousands of working men who stand before me in this hall, and who are included in this attack—I deny it. (Cheers.) In the name of the gentlemen who stand around me on this platform, who countenance our proceedings, who are identified with them, and who are included in this attack—I deny it. (Renewed cheering.) In the name of the great body of merchants, manufacturers, traders, and others in different parts of the country, identified with us, and who are included in this attack—I deny it. (Continued cheering) . . . And, lastly, in the name of two thousand ministers of religion—(loud and reiterated cheering)—who have left their sacred calling that they might lend their aid in obtaining bread for the hungry, and clothing for the naked, and who are included in the attack—I deny it. (Renewed cheers.) And, finally, I hurl back the calumny upon whoever may choose to utter it, as a most atrocious, most wilful, and most audacious falsehood." (Loud and long-continued cheering.)

The hall, during this effective piece of rhetoric, presented an extraordinary scene of excitement, which lasted some time after the speaker had resumed his seat. The meeting was then addressed by several gentlemen, among whom was Mr. John Bright, and an address to Mr. Cobden was unanimously voted. The main purport of this address was summarised in the following paragraph extracted from it:—" Fortified by the approbation of your own conscience and by that of a vast portion of your fellow-countrymen, who have watched your career with intense and increasing interest, you can well afford to despise the assaults and calumnies with which the abettors of monopoly seek to turn you from the prosecution of the great work to which you have so nobly devoted yourself."

On the 1st of March a meeting was held in London, at the Crown and Anchor tavern, which was so overcrowded that it became a matter of necessity to provide some far more spacious area for future meetings. The use of Exeter Hall was applied for but refused.

1843. Finally, Drury Lane Theatre was engaged for one night a week during the Lent season; and the first meeting of the League was held there on the evening of Wednesday, March 15th.

A history of the Free-Trade movement in England would be utterly incomplete if it did not include some account of the large, numerous, and influential public meetings which were either held by the Anti-Corn-Law League themselves, or convened in furtherance of their views. It was through the medium of these assemblages chiefly that public opinion made its voice heard, which, swelling louder and louder, commanded attention and enforced respect. The continued efforts of the League had placed the subject of Free Trade under such a fierce blaze of public discussion and inquiry, that the old commonplaces, sophisms, and "musty phrases" by which it had so long been obscured, were vaporised and cleared away; and those truths which, till then, had been known to only a few political economists, became widely prevalent and popular.

Indeed, hardly an attempt was made to controvert them by reasoning. The Protectionist journals complained bitterly that the Parliamentary representatives of the old system allowed the statements and arguments of the Free Traders to pass unrefuted in the House, and that, content with being victorious in the divisions, they allowed their opponents to triumph in the debates. It was this gradual and ever-growing conversion of public opinion to the principles of commercial freedom that led to their practical adoption, for it was not the people alone that were converted, but numerous proselytes were also made among legislators and statesmen. By whom, and in what way these conversions were effected it is the object of this history to record. Honour both to the converts and to the converters! If to the latter belongs the merit of initiating the movement, the former deserve credit for their brave repudiation of former errors and their manly recognition of the truth. Free-Trade policy is simply principle reduced to practice; but its adoption by responsible statesmen required not only thorough conviction, but also the moral courage to act up to it.

The first meeting at Drury Lane Theatre was, to use a stage term, an "overflow." Pit, boxes, and gallery—all were crowded; and never did the efforts of the most finished performer on those boards elicit such enthusiastic applause as that which greeted the appearance of George Wilson, the chairman of the League, or the speeches of Messrs. Cobden and Bright, "their first appearance on that stage." These meetings were continued weekly till the middle of April, when Mr. Macready, the lessee, was prohibited by the Shareholders' Committee from letting the theatre for political purposes. The audiences had gone on increasing both in numbers and in earnestness, and the difficulty now was to find some enclosed area of sufficient dimensions to contain the thousands who sought admittance. This want was never thoroughly supplied. The transference of the Manchester Free Trade Hall bodily to London could alone have met the requirement.

We pass rapidly over the motions made in Parliament by Mr. Ward for a Committee to inquire into

1843. the burdens, if any, which specially affect the landed interest, and by Mr. Ricardo deprecating any postponement in the remission of our import duties, with a view to negotiations for reciprocity. They were negatived by large majorities, but they elicited declarations from Sir Robert Peel which proved his unqualified adherence to the principles of Free Trade, though he still, for the present, threw the weight of his influence into the opposite scale. Referring to commercial treaties then in course of negotiation, he said :—" We have reserved many articles from immediate reduction in the hope that ere long we may attain . . . increased facilities for our exports in return. At the same time, I am bound to say that it is for our interest to buy cheap, whether other countries will buy cheap or no. . . If we find that our example is not followed, if we find that other nations, instead of reducing the duties on our manufactures, resort to the impolicy of increasing them, this ought not, in my opinion, to operate as a discouragement to us to act on those principles which we believe to be sound. . . . If the Brazilians choose to pay an artificially high price for cotton and woollen cloths, that is no reason why we should pay a high price for sugar and coffee."

We now come to the debate of the Session—that on Mr. Villiers' annual motion. On the 13th May he moved—" That the House should resolve itself into a Committee for the purpose of considering the duties affecting the importation of foreign corn, with the view to their immediate abolition." Mr. Gladstone opposed the motion in an able speech. He deprecated fresh changes in the Corn Laws, until the effect of the change recently made had been developed. He referred to the great fall in the price of wheat, which had followed the last abundant harvest. He compared the prices then current with those of 1835, "the cheapest of the present generation." The price of wheat in May, 1835, was 39s. 2d., in May, 1843, 46s. 4d. . . . He referred to the low prices of wheat prevailing in America. "A person sent," he said, "to the Western States by one of the corn houses in this country, to investigate the state of the harvest last year, and the probable quantities of wheat and flour that might be exported from the Mississippi, in case of an opening into this country by a repeal of the Corn Laws, reported that the harvest last year was greater than was ever known before; the price at New Orleans was likely to be 21s. to 24s. per quarter, and the quantity 350,000 quarters. . . . I am satisfied that the motion could not be adopted without a great action upon the currency. There was now a drain of gold on this country, which had sent £3,000,000 to America since the commencement of the present year; and I am afraid that any considerable importation of foreign corn must be paid for in bullion."

We cannot refrain from a few words of parenthetical remark on the two facts stated by Mr. Gladstone. Let us note—1. How ludicrously small was the quantity of wheat which it was estimated that America could send us in 1843, compared with what she actually did send us in 1879. At the former period, Tamboff was the farmer's *bête noire*; Chicago was not dreamt of.

1843. Oh, the fallibility of human previsions! 2. America, during the first five months of 1843, drained us of gold to the extent of £3,000,000, at the time when we were not taking a shilling's-worth of her bread-stuffs. Curious! It appears, then, that although we could prevent foreign goods from coming in, we could not prevent English gold from going out. How was it that it escaped from us when Protection reigned supreme, and every device was used to export much and import little?

But to proceed. The more clear-sighted of the Protectionist members gave free vent to their feelings of distrust and uneasiness as to the Free-Trade doctrines entertained and avowed by some of the Ministers. True that, so far, the practical outcome of such doctrines had only been the substitution of one form of sliding-scale for another, both sufficiently protective, and the reduction of duties on miscellaneous articles of minor importance. But where was the line to be drawn? The great evil of the Ministerial adhesion to abstract principles was the danger of their acting upon them. If they did so, what would become of the landed interests, the vested interests, the protected interests, the corporate interests, and the rest of the time-honoured institutions of the country? Mr. Blackstone was the organ representing the views of the uncompromising agricultural party, and he expressed them, if not with logical force, at least with ingenuous simplicity. "The agriculturists," he exclaimed, "looked to the future in a state of the utmost despair, and conceived that there was so much doubt as to the line of conduct which Her Majesty's Ministers would pursue hereafter, that they would rather at once see the end come—(loud cheering from Opposition members)—than wait in suspense and die by inches." (Continued cheers.)

Another great agricultural authority, and a member of the Ministry, Sir Edward Knatchbull, contended that, "If Free-Trade were applied in this particular case, it must be so generally and universally—(loud Opposition cheers)—but this I regard as impracticable. If applied in the case of land, its peculiar burdens must be taken into consideration; among which I reckon pecuniary liabilities and provisions for younger children." This unfortunate appeal *ad misericordiam* was mercilessly dissected by Lord John Russell, who followed next, and who said :—"The right honourable gentleman, a Cabinet Minister, stated as one reason why they should keep up the present law, that they might provide by their marriage-settlements for the younger members of their families." Here Sir Edward Knatchbull interposed with a scarcely-intelligible explanation. Lord John Russell proceeded :—"I understand that to mean, not that the Corn Law ought to remain, but that, if it were removed, then it would be the duty of Parliament to consider what was the amount of compensation to be given to those gentlemen who were interested in maintaining the Corn Law. If it was abolished, it was said that then there was to be a case of compensation, something like that to the slave-owners." In conclusion, Lord John Russell announced his intention to vote against the motion, because it pledged him to the total abolition of all duties on corn, whereas he was in favour of a moderate fixed duty.

1843.   Richard Cobden made a forcible speech, in which he pointed out that it was not the farmers who benefited by the exclusion of foreign corn. On the contrary they were ruined by the excessive fluctuations which it occasioned; the rents being assessed on the high prices of scarcity years, and being exacted in spite of the low prices of abundant years. The capital of the farmer was wasting away, because the money which should go to pay labour went to pay rents. "Your rents!" emphatically added Mr. Cobden, addressing the agricultural members opposite to him. He concluded a speech more distinguished for its terse and vigorous, than for its ornate or conciliatory language, amid loud clamour from the country gentlemen, who were not accustomed to such plain speaking and to such scathing denunciations of the evils of protective duties.

The debate lasted five nights, and elicited a multitude of speeches, almost duplicates of each other in various forms of tediousness. Of course the motion was lost by a large majority. It only enlisted in its favour the votes of those thorough Free Traders who advocated total and immediate repeal of all duties on corn, and who numbered 125; while against it were recorded the votes of all the Conservatives and most of the Whigs, who collectively numbered 381.

As we before observed, the Protectionist papers were dissatisfied with the lack of argumentative and rhetorical power exhibited by their Parliamentary representatives. The following remarks are from the *Morning Post*:—"Melancholy was the exhibition in the House of Commons on Monday. Mr. Cobden was the hero of the night. Towards the close of the debate he rose in his place and hurled at the heads of the Parliamentary landowners of England those calumnies and taunts which constitute the staple of his addresses to farmers. The taunts were not retorted. The calumnies were not repelled. No; the representatives of the industrial interests of the British Empire quailed before the founder and leader of the Anti-Corn-Law League. They winced under his sarcasms. They listened in speechless terror to his denunciations. No man among them dared to grapple with the arch enemy of English industry. . . . Melancholy was it to witness, on Monday, the landowners of England, the representatives by blood of the Norman chivalry, the representatives by election of the industrial interests of the Empire, shrinking under the blows aimed at them by a Manchester money-grubber." We can fancy Richard Cobden reading such attacks on himself with a grim smile of complacency. He had no objection to be reviled provided he were successful; and the bitterness of his opponents afforded the best proof that his blows had struck home.

Shortly after the debate on Mr. Villiers' motion, Lord Stanley, who was Secretary for the Colonies, brought forward a measure which aggravated the discontent of the agricultural party. It proposed to admit into the United Kingdom wheat from Canada at a duty of one shilling per quarter, provided the Canadian Legislature imposed a duty of three shillings per quarter on wheat imported into Canada from foreign countries. It was opposed by the advocates of the landed interest, as being an infringement on the

1843. protective principle of the Corn Laws, and a disturbance of the settlement recently come to in respect to them. American wheat would be smuggled into Canada, and a quantity of foreign wheat would be let in at one shilling duty, to the detriment of the English producer.

The Whigs opposed it on a variety of minor pleas, some of which, viewed with our present lights, appear curious. For instance, Mr. Roebuck argued that as Canada could not grow enough wheat for herself, and was an importing country, the three-shilling duty would raise the price of wheat to the Canadian consumers; and he would therefore oppose the measure. It is worth noting that in 1879 we imported from British North America (which in 1843 did not grow wheat enough for home consumption) wheat to the value of £2,560,000! The measure was carried through its various phases by large majorities in both Houses of Parliament, and speedily became law.

CHAPTER VIII
(1843.)

The City of Durham sends Mr. John Bright to Parliament—Proceedings of the Anti-Corn-Law League, which proposes to raise £100,000.

THE incessant labours of Mr. Cobden in the House of Commons did not prevent him from pursuing his crusade among the farmers, with the view of securing their adhesion to the principles of Free Trade, and removing from their minds the impression that they were benefited by the Corn Laws. Either he or Mr.

John Bright, sometimes both, assisted by Mr. R. R. Moore and others, during the months of May and June alone, addressed farmers' meetings at the following places — Aylesbury, Bedford, Cambridge, Colchester, Guildford, Hertford, Huntingdon, Lewes, Lincoln, Maidstone, Rye, Uxbridge, and Winchester. The mission was attended with complete success. The majority of the farmers soon became convinced that it was a landlords' question, not a farmers' question—that the enormous fluctuations in the value of wheat, resulting from a dependence on the harvests of one country instead of the harvests of the world, were very injurious to the farmer, whose rents were based on the higher prices—that the farmers' safety is in steadiness of prices, high or low, on the average of which rents would finally be based—and that cheap bread meant national prosperity, attended by an increase of his customers, the bread-eaters. The minds of the listeners were aroused and quickened by these eloquent appeals to their reason, and in this, as well as in many other ways, the Free-Trade agitation proved a great educational as well as a great political movement.

On the 25th of July an event occurred which greatly strengthened the hands of Richard Cobden, by giving him a parliamentary coadjutor of extraordinary ability, vigour, and eloquence. Mr. John Bright was elected member for Durham, in lieu of Lord Dungannon unseated for bribery. This would be the proper place to attempt a sketch of the man who bore so prominent a part in the emancipation of his country from a vicious commercial policy, were our

1843. pen not restrained by the fact of his presence still among us as a prominent and influential statesman. No career can be fittingly described till it is ended. The finishing touches cannot be given to the delineation of a character as long as the data requisite for its full appreciation are incomplete. But we may perhaps be permitted to refer briefly to a few of Mr. Bright's distinctive characteristics; to his immutable fidelity to the principles with which he started into public life, for we are not aware of one from which he has swerved a hair's-breadth; to the sincerity of his utterances, for his most inveterate enemies, while taxing his speeches with too often displaying indiscretion, acrimony, and superfluous bitterness of personal invective, have never charged him with dissimulation or questioned his honesty of purpose; to the splendour of his eloquence, fervid, copious, manly, and stirring the hearts of his hearers because it comes straight from his own; to the spirited tenacity with which he has, again and again, stood almost alone in the advocacy of a forlorn cause, and bravely breasted the tide of adverse public opinion; and to the touching affection that he ever bore, through many years of joint political action, to his illustrious fellow-labourer, colleague and friend, Richard Cobden.

The next step in the direction of Free Trade taken by the Peel Ministry was the repeal of the restrictions which existed on the exportation of machinery. Mr. Gladstone, on bringing in a bill for this purpose, remarked that the prohibition to export machinery originated in the belief that if foreigners were debarred from getting it, the goods to be made by it would be produced in this country and our trade increased. The law had proved nugatory, as the machinery was exported in detached pieces. The effect of the law had been simply to enhance the cost of British machinery to the foreign purchaser, and to throw the manufacture into the hands of the Belgians, whose trade in it had largely increased. The Free Traders of course gave to the measure their hearty support, and as they represented the mill and factory owners whose interests were supposed to be involved, it passed almost unanimously.

Parliament was prorogued on the 24th of August by the Queen in person, after a protracted session, during which the actual legislative work done only bore a small proportion to the amount of time and toil devoted to discussion.

Soon afterwards the Anti-Corn-Law League commenced their preparations for the next campaign. Their first step was to issue a report stating what work had been performed during the year. To sum it up briefly, we find that the number of tracts and stamped publications issued and distributed by the Council during that period amounted to 9,026,000, weighing, in the aggregate, upwards of 100 tons—the lecturers employed, 14 in number, had delivered 650 lectures in 59 counties through England, Wales, and Scotland—deputations had been sent to 156 public meetings in counties and boroughs—the total expenditure had been £47,814 3s. 9d.—and the balance in hand on the 9th Sept. was £2,476 10s. 3d.

The three chief features in the programme they now put forth were :—1. To raise a fund of £100,000;

1843. 2. To engage Covent Garden theatre for fifty nights, at a rent of £3,000; 3. To devote £10,000 to the publication and distribution of a full-sized weekly newspaper to be called *The League*. A bold and comprehensive scheme, which only the enthusiasm of deep conviction could have conceived, and only the efforts of combined pluck and talent could have carried out. Here was a handful of men who, by the legitimate agency of instruction, persuasion, and exhortation, had rallied round them a force of public opinion which enabled them to enlarge their sphere of agitation to the extent now proposed. Truly, a notable performance of the difficult feat of "converting a minority into a majority!"

On the 28th September the first public meeting convened by the League at Covent Garden Theatre took place. Mr. George Wilson, as permanent chairman, presided. Every part of the vast area was crowded to excess. Richard Cobden, and after him Mr. Bright, spoke, and their two admirable and effective speeches elicited enthusiastic applause. There then came forward a round-faced, obese man, of small stature, whom (if you avoided looking at his eyes), you might take to be a person slow of comprehension and slow of utterance—a sleek, satisfied, perhaps sensual person—a calm, patient, and somewhat lethargic man. The only thing remarkable about him (always excepting his eyes) was a mass of long, thick, black hair, which waved over his neck and shoulders. This man spoke, and the vast audience was thrilled by his wonderful eloquence. It was W. J. Fox, the Unitarian Minister, and afterwards member for Oldham. The moment he began to speak he seemed another man. His large brown eyes flashed fire, and his impressive gestures imparted dignity to his stature. His voice displayed a combination of power and sweetness, not surpassed even by the mellow bass tones of Daniel O'Connell in his prime. His command of language seemed unlimited, for he was never at a loss, not only for a word, but for the right word. Not argumentative and persuasive like Cobden, or natural and forcible as Mr. Bright, his *forte* lay rather in appealing to the emotions of his audience, and in this branch of the oratorical art his power was irresistible. An eye-witness * says : "So beautifully articulated was every syllable, that his stage-whisper might have been heard at the farthest extremity of the gallery. The matter was excellent; abounding with neatly-pointed epigram, cutting sarcasm, withering denunciation, and argument condensed and urged with laconic force. . . . The speech read well; but the reader could have no conception of its effect as delivered, with a beauty of elocution, which Macready, on those same boards, might have envied. The effect, when he called on his hearers to bind themselves in a solemn league never to cease their labours till the Corn Laws were abolished, was electrical, thousands starting on their feet, with arms extended, as if ready to swear extinction to monopoly."

About this time the League was strengthened by the adhesion of two representative men. Mr. Samuel Jones Loyd, afterwards Lord Overstone, sent in a subscription to their funds of £50. This gentleman

* Prentice. "History of the Anti-Corn-Law League."

1843. was distinguished in the financial circles of the City for his opulence, caution, and ability; and his accession exercised great influence over the minds of the timid and wavering. Simultaneously a great landowner, Earl Fitzwilliam, in company with Richard Cobden and Mr. Bright, attended a public meeting at Doncaster, where, in an able speech, he moved a resolution that all protective duties should be promptly abolished, which was carried by an immense majority. That the League was working upwards as well as downwards, and that, starting as it did from the middle class, it was extending its sway among the higher as well as the lower strata of society, was evident from these accessions to its ranks.

An additional proof was afforded at about the same time of the increasing popularity of Free-Trade principles, by the suffrages of the City of London. A vacancy having occurred in the representation of the City, two candidates presented themselves: Mr. Baring, strong in himself from his name, position, and talents, who was supported by the Ministerial and Conservative party; and Mr. Pattison, the Liberal and Free-Trade candidate, who was taunted with being the nominee of the League. The contest was severe, but Mr. Pattison was elected by a majority of 345. This victory was hailed as a great triumph for the Free-Trade party, and at the ensuing weekly League meeting in Covent Garden Theatre, a crowded and enthusiastic assemblage unanimously voted a congratulatory address to the citizens of London.

Nor did the supporters of the League shrink from more severe and substantial tests of their sincerity and earnestness. The hundred-thousand-pound fund had to be raised. Public meetings were held in a great number of places, for the purpose of inviting and receiving subscriptions. At that held in Manchester on the 14th of November, £12,000 was subscribed in an hour and a half. Several persons gave £500 each. That the ladies were hearty and effective helpmates to the cause was manifested in many various ways. The following is one example. Archibald Prentice, the historian of the League, and who minutely chronicled the proceedings *quorum pars magna fuit*, writes: "Mr. Brooks called upon Mr. Robert Ashton a few days ago to ask him to attend the meeting. He found him sitting with his lady, and solicited his subscription to the fund. 'I gave you £100 last year, and shall give you £200 now,' was the answer. 'Give him £500, Robert,' was the quiet suggestion of the lady; and Mr. Ashton, who is worthy of such a wife, at once assented."

In most other districts similar munificence and self-sacrifice was displayed, and it soon became apparent that the large sum at which the country's contributions had been assessed by the League would be obtained. As this emerged from a possibility into a fact, public opinion was deeply impressed by such an exhibition of unflinching vigour and latent power, and its conclusions found a lively exponent in a leading article which appeared in the *Times* of the 18th of November. We give a few extracts. "The League is a great fact. It would be foolish, nay, rash, to deny its importance. . . . It demonstrates the hardy strength of purpose, the indomitable will by which

1843. Englishmen working together for a great object are armed and animated. It is a great fact that at one meeting at Manchester, more than forty manufacturers should subscribe on the spot, each at least £100, some £300, some £400, some £500, for the advancement of a measure which, right or wrong, just or unjust, expedient or injurious, they at least believe it to be their duty, or their interest, or both, to advance in every possible way. These are facts important and worthy of consideration. No moralist can disregard them; no politician can sneer at them; no statesman can undervalue them. He who collects opinions must chronicle them. He who frames laws must, to some extent, consult them. . . . The League may be a hypocrite, a great deceiver, a huge Trojan horse of sedition. Be it so; but we answer, the League exists. . . . A new power has arisen in the state, and maids and matrons flock to theatres, as though it were but 'a new translation from the French.' Let no man say that we are blind to the possible mischiefs of such a state of things. We acknowledge that we dislike gregarious collections of cant and cotton men. We cannot but know that, whatever be the end of this agitation, it will expire only to bequeath its violence and its turbulence to some successor."

This reluctant recognition of "a new power in the state" created no little sensation. The Ministerial papers deprecated the admission while they at the same time joined in it. But they attributed the formidable dimensions which the League had attained, less to its own efforts and merits, than to the silence and apathy of the landowners whose interests were assailed, and to the doubtful attitude assumed by the political chiefs of the party. The *Morning Herald* commenting on the article in the *Times* thus expressed itself:—" That confederacy (the League) is powerful: its inherent power is increased by the supineness of those great interests it assaults ; and its ultimate success is certain, unless vigour and unanimity be re-infused into the Conservative party. The sincerity of its leading men is testified by their subscriptions; and the determination of its moving men is certified by their indomitable perseverance, their incessant activity, and their remorseless unscrupulousness." The *Morning Post*, equally vehement but more personal, alludes pointedly in the following paragraph to Sir Robert Peel:—" The antagonist influence which they (the League) had to overthrow was little better than a *vis inertiæ*, which might be overcome by great activity and great effrontery. They discovered that the landed interest was not likely to be defended by the owners of land with such weapons as in these days prevail, and that they had placed their championship in the hands of political leaders, who were more likely to give up the battle upon a fair excuse, than to fight it out from a sense of duty."

No wonder that the statesman whose duty it was to strive for the welfare of a nation, and the journalist whose mission it was to uphold the interests of a party, were soon at variance. The greater the advance each made in his prescribed path, the greater became their divergence. The only conditions on which they could keep together were, that Sir Robert Peel should

1844. ignore his newly-formed convictions, act upon principles of which he had discovered the fallacy, and "to party give up what was meant for mankind." Fortunately for the country and for himself, he chose the "better part."

CHAPTER IX.
(1844.)
Meetings of the Anti-Corn-Law League—The Budget Exhibits a Surplus—Fresh Import-duty Reductions—Ministers Out-voted on the Sugar Question—Sir Robert Peel induces the House to Rescind the Vote—The League at Work on the Voting Registers.

THE year 1844 opened under favourable auspices. An abundant harvest, after a cycle of bad ones, had infused fresh life and vigour into the country. Trade had partially revived, increased demand for labour had diminished pauperism and raised wages, the price of wheat was 52s. to 54s. per quarter instead of the high prices of recent years, bread was proportionately cheaper, and incipient prosperity had allayed discontent. This period of reaction was the crucial test by which the soundness of the Free-Trade movement was to be tried. If it was ephemeral, and owed its existence merely to the temporary distress of the people, it must now collapse. But if founded on principle, and on a legitimate demand for the adaptation of scientific truths to our commercial policy, it would survive, and pursue its career. We shall see that it did survive, and that its career only closed with its triumph.

On the first day of the new year the Marquis of Westminster wrote a letter to George Wilson, the

Chairman of the League, congratulating that body on its success, inciting it to fresh exertions, and enclosing a cheque for £500, as a contribution to its funds. A new year's gift of good augury! During the month of January a multitude of meetings were held throughout the country, for the two purposes of collecting money and of keeping the subject fresh in the minds of the people. At as many of these meetings as it was physically possible for them to attend, Messrs. Cobden and Bright delivered addresses, sometimes assisted, at other times replaced, by Colonel P. Thompson, C. P. Villiers, R. R. Moore, W. J. Fox, and others.

One of the most enthusiastic of these meetings was that held at Wakefield, on the 31st of January, at which Lord Morpeth spoke at some length, and proclaimed his adhesion to the principles of the League, but at the same time confessed his hankering for a small—just a mere trifle of—fixed duty on corn. The audience rapturously welcomed his co-operation, but protested against the slightest abatement from total repeal.

On the 1st of February Parliament was opened by the Queen in person, with the customary solemnities. The Speech, delivered with her usual clearness of utterance and grace of manner, was, on all topics save that of Ireland, couched in congratulatory language, and it was replied to by Parliament in a responsive strain of cheerfulness. Two amendments to the Address, moved by Sharman Crawford and Joseph Hume, found but few supporters.

In the course of the debate, Lord John Russell said,

1844. in reference to the sliding scale of duties on corn: "With respect to almost all articles of commerce, we adopt a moderate duty; but with respect to corn, an article in which the great majority of both Houses of Parliament are pecuniarily interested, we levy a duty of forty per cent." This hit elicited loud applause from the Opposition, but only drew forth from Sir Robert Peel the following declaration:— "The experience we have had of the present (Corn) law has not shaken my preference for a graduated duty; and although I consider it inconsistent with my duty to make engagements for adherence to existing laws under all circumstances, in order to conciliate support, I can say that the Government have never contemplated, and do not contemplate, any alteration in the existing law." This announcement was received by the landed interest with exultation tempered by distrust, and by the Free Traders with displeasure modified by incredulity. Neither party believed that the present code was a final settlement, and the apprehensions of the former pointed in the same direction as the hopes of the latter.

It was, however, clear from Sir Robert Peel's words that, whatever might be his ulterior policy, he would, during this session at least, resist any change in the existing Corn Law. The leaders of the Free-Trade party felt, therefore, that while it was a hopeless task to act on the Ministers through the House, their policy was to act on both by steady and continuous pressure from without. They had asked the country for £100,000 and they were getting it fast. Their newspaper, *The League*, had reached a weekly circulation of 15,000 copies, and was disseminating their principles far and wide; and their periodical meetings at Covent Garden Theatre were attended by crowds of enthusiastic listeners.

They did not nevertheless relax their efforts in Parliament, and on the 12th of March Mr. Cobden moved for a committee "to inquire into the effects of protective duties on agricultural tenants and labourers." In his speech he argued that free imports of wheat would not lower prices to the extent of throwing land out of cultivation—that the proportion of rent to the other expenses of producing wheat was nearly one half—that when the price of corn was highest, wages were lowest, and employment scarcest. He concluded by asking, "On what ground was such a committee to be refused? The danger of excitement? There will be much more excitement occasioned by the refusal than by the concession of it." It was opposed by Mr. Gladstone, and negatived by a majority of 91.

The budget was brought forward by Mr. Goulburn on the 29th April, and exhibited some very favourable features. The revenue had exceeded the estimates by £2,700,000; and instead of the deficiencies which of late years had continuously characterised the national balance-sheet, this lucky Chancellor of the Exchequer boasted a surplus. Having got it, however, he did not appear at all disposed to part with more of it than he could help, and he limited his tax-remissions to some reduction of the duties on the following articles:—Glass, vinegar, currants, coffee, marine insurance, and wool, upon the aggregate of which

1844 the amount of duty to be remitted would be £387,000 a year. He also gave notice that he would later on propose a separate measure concerning the sugar duties. The Opposition members contented themselves for the present with protesting against the niggardly amount of the intended remissions, conceiving that the sugar question would afford them a more favourable battle-field on which to try conclusions with the Ministry. The event justified their strategy, for the contest was a severe one, and proved nearly fatal to the Peel administration.

On the 3rd of June Mr. Goulburn moved that the duties on sugar, which then stood at 24s. per cwt. on the sugar of British possessions, and at 63s. on all foreign sugar, should henceforth stand at 24s. per cwt. on the sugar of British possessions, 63s. per cwt. on foreign sugar produced by slave labour, and 34s. per cwt. on foreign sugar produced by free labour. This measure was a decided step in the direction of Free Trade, since, whereas our colonial sugars had hitherto been protected against all foreign sugar by a difference in duty of 39s. per cwt., it was now proposed to reduce that protection, in case of foreign sugar produced by free labour, to a difference in duty of only 10s. per cwt. Substantially it was a reduction of 29s. per cwt. on the duty levied on the sugars of China, Java, Manilla, and other free-labour countries. Lord John Russell moved as an amendment that the duty on all foreign sugar be reduced to 34s., whether produced by slave labour or not. A majority of 69 negatived this amendment. It did not attract a single deserter from the Ministerial camp. The blow which staggered the Government came from one of its own supporters.

On the 14th of June Mr. P. Miles moved, in committee, that the Government proposal be modified as follows :—The duty on British colonial sugar to be reduced to 20s.; that on the sugars of China, Java, and Manilla to 30s., except when imported at a certain degree of refinement, and then to be 34s. This proposition was resisted by Mr. Goulburn, and supported by the Opposition. But Mr. Miles and his followers stood their ground, and reinforced by their unwonted allies, the Liberal party, placed the Government in a minority of 20. Thereupon the committee adjourned to the 17th, and meanwhile speculation was rife as to the course which Ministers would adopt.

On the 17th Sir Robert Peel declared that they must adhere to their own measure, and announced, in delicate but significant language, his intention to resign unless the House reversed its previous decision. He concluded by saying that "in certain of their measures the Government had failed to obtain the approbation of some whose support they most valued. He could not profess that they were prepared to purchase that approbation at the price of refraining from the policy which they deemed essential to the welfare of the country." An animated debate ensued. Indignant protests were made against a course which, it was said, would lower the character of the House throughout the country. Mr. Disraeli was particularly severe. He referred to the position in which they were placed as one "which no member of this House, whether he be on this, or on the Opposition side, can describe as other than degrading to us all. . . The right hon. gentleman came forward with a detestation of slavery in every place—except in the benches behind him. . . . He deserved a better position than one that could only be retained by menacing his friends and cringing to his opponents." Lord Howick supported the 20s. against the 24s. duty. "It was," he said, "quite a new doctrine that the Government were entitled to go out whenever their supporters differed from them. At that rate, all which the House of Commons would have to do would be to pass a vote of confidence at the beginning of the Session and then quietly to disperse to their homes. . . . . It was clear that the Ministers' followers supported them not because they liked them but because they disliked still more the persons likely to succeed them." On a division, Ministers obtained a majority of 22.

The determined attitude assumed at this crisis by Sir Robert Peel strengthened and consolidated his power. The *ultra* Protectionists discovered that mutiny was worse than useless. They must either follow their chief, or place themselves at the mercy of their foes. They might subvert the Ministry, but were powerless to guide its course. To be beguiled smoothly and gradually in the direction of Free Trade by a professed friend, bad as it was, seemed better than to be dragged violently into it by the sudden and precipitate action of an avowed enemy. They therefore, with few exceptions, quietly subsided into silent subordination.

It is not within the scope of this work to do more

than briefly allude to a measure which Sir Robert Peel introduced about this time, and which reflects the greatest credit on his ability as a financier, an economist, and a statesman. We allude to his renewal of the Bank Charter and to the banking and monetary regulations incorporated in it. His speech on the occasion showed not only how well he understood the question himself, but how well he could make it understood by others. The subject is inherently dry, tedious, and complicated, but, under his treatment, it became positively interesting and attractive.

Mr. Villiers, on the 25th of June, brought forward his annual motion against the Corn Laws in a somewhat novel shape. He proposed a series of resolutions, of which we give the substance. "That it appears by a recent census that the people of this country are rapidly increasing in number . . ." that a large proportion of her Majesty's subjects are insufficiently provided with the first necessaries of life. That, nevertheless, a corn law is in force which restricts the supply of food, and thereby lessens its abundance. That any such restriction . . . is indefensible in principle, injurious in operation, and ought to be abolished." The debate elicited hardly any new feature of interest. It was the same old story. The Free Traders proclaimed the theory, and advocated the adoption of Free Trade; the Protectionists vigorously opposed both; and the Ministers, while admitting the abstract theory, resisted its adoption, except "in the proper degree," "at the proper time," and "under proper conditions." The result was of course that, those who wanted practice to conform to theory were

1844. largely out-voted by a coalition between those who advocated theory without practice and those who rejected both.

Hardly any further action was taken during this Session in regard to Free-Trade measures. Lord John Russell raised a debate on the 9th of August on the condition of the country, but beyond an interchange of bitter civilities between him and the Prime Minister, it led to no result; and on the 5th of September Parliament was prorogued.

There was now every promise of another abundant harvest, which would, if realised, accelerate the improvement which was already visible in almost every branch of trade. A more cheerful tone prevailed among all classes of the community but one. The national revenue had recovered with unexpected elasticity, and not only was the previous year's deficiency of £2,400,000 cleared off, but a large surplus remained. The condition of the working classes had undergone considerable amelioration, except in the case of the agricultural labourers. What with heavy rents based on high prices and comparatively low prices consequent upon a good harvest, farmers were sorely tried, and they cut down the wages of their men to the utmost endurable point. In many districts the farm-labourers, ignorant and torpid, had to submit to a pittance of 5s., 6s., or 7s. per week, and their misery drove them into savage despair. Rick-burning and incendiarism in various forms became rife in the counties of Suffolk and Norfolk, and the agricultural section of the empire exhibited a striking exception to the universal improvement. In startling contrast to this fact was another fact—that they were by far the most highly protected class in the country.

The meetings held at this period by the Anti-Corn-Law League were not so numerous as in former years, and the landlords gave exultant expression to their belief that its leaders were relaxing in their efforts and despairing of success. That hateful agitation, they thought and said, can only flourish amid the gloom and irritation of calamity and distress, and must collapse in the presence of national prosperity. But they were mistaken. The energies of the League had by no means drooped, but had simply been directed into a fresh channel. They had set to work upon the voting registers, and by urging new claims as well as by revising old ones, had secured a large increase in the votes of their party, and thus paved the way for the success of their candidates at the next election. For several months, from July to October, the League and its agents were engaged, quietly, unobtrusively, but effectually, in this important work.

At a crowded meeting held on the 24th of October, in the Manchester Free Trade Hall, the chairman, Mr. G. Wilson, gave a detailed report of their labours in this direction, and summed up by saying, " I have in my hand a list of returns for 70 out of the 140 boroughs over which the League has exercised some influence, and of these there are 68 in which there has been a clear gain upon the registration; in some a great gain, but less or more in all. . . . We have concentrated our energies on these points. . . Our opponents may gather from the results whether the

1844. League has been dead or slumbering, and they will accordingly derive what consolation they may from them." Richard Cobden followed in a stirring speech, wherein he strongly exhorted all those who could afford to invest £50 or £60 in land to do so, as that would confer on them a vote for the county.

At an overflowing meeting held at Covent Garden Theatre on the 12th of December, Mr. John Bright addressed the assemblage in a strain of impassioned eloquence which greatly moved his hearers. His peroration was as follows:— "This freedom for which you struggle is the freedom to live; it is the right to 'eat your bread by the sweat of your brow.' It is the freedom which was given to you even in the primeval curse; and shall man make that curse more bitter to his fellow man? No; instead of despairing, I have more confidence and faith than ever. I believe that those old delusions and superstitions which, like verminous and polluted rags, have disfigured the fair form of this country's greatness, are now fast dropping away. I think I behold the dawn of a brighter day; all around are the elements of a mighty movement. We stand as on the very threshold of a new career; and we may say that this League—this great and growing confederacy of those who love justice and hate oppression—has scattered broadcast throughout the land seed from which shall spring forth ere long an abundant, a glorious harvest of true greatness for our country, and of permanent happiness for mankind." Are these the words of men despairing of their cause, or contemplating retirement from the contest?

CHAPTER X.

(1845.)

State of Parties at the Opening of Parliament—Large Reductions in the Import Duties—Dissatisfaction of the Protectionist Party—Mr. Disraeli's Philippics—Anti-Corn-Law League Bazaar at Covent Garden Theatre—Mr. Villiers' Annual Motion.

As a prelude to the struggles which were to mark the eventful year 1845, a great meeting was held, on the 8th of January, in the Manchester Free Trade Hall. It was succeeded by another in Covent Garden Theatre, London, and by a third crowded and enthusiastic gathering at Manchester, besides numerous others at Liverpool, Durham, and several parts of the country. These meetings were addressed by various members of the League, and by none more frequently or more effectually than by Richard Cobden, J. Bright, and W. J. Fox. With wonderful fertility of device, they were continually introducing into their speeches new topics in illustration of their theme, or placing old arguments in new lights, or seizing upon some novelty of the day and pressing it into their service.

But however great the versatility of the speakers and the variety of treatment which they gave to their subject, all their efforts converged towards one focus, and the burden was still the same, viz., "Free Trade is essential to our prosperity, and there must be neither rest nor respite till we get it." And indeed it was evident, even to their adversaries, that each year was bringing them nearer to that result. True, that, in spite of public favour and popular support, they were largely out-voted in both Houses of Parlia-

1845. ment. But their opponents no longer formed a compact body. The process of disintegration had set in. One part was dropping away from the other, and the triumph of the Free Traders over a disunited and discouraged party was only a question of time. Even if the present Parliament did remain obdurate, it could only last two or three years longer, and a new House of Commons would inaugurate a new commercial policy. But there proved no necessity for waiting so long; and, as we shall see, a microscopic fungus on the tissue of the potato plant hastened the crisis and prematurely brought on the final struggle.

In happy ignorance of the impending calamity, the contending parties made their preparations for the ensuing campaign. There were, in respect to our fiscal policy, four distinct sections in the House of Commons. The Protectionists, ostensibly led by such mediocre persons as P. Miles and G. Bankes, but in reality headed by Lord Stanley and Mr. B. Disraeli, two men of rare abilities, who, moving rapidly to the front, subsequently reached the highest pinnacle of political power; the Ministerial party, of which the ruling spirits were Sir Robert Peel and Mr. W. E. Gladstone; the Moderate Liberals, represented by Lord John Russell and Lord Palmerston; and the Free Traders, whom the genius of Richard Cobden and John Bright had organised into a compact and powerful phalanx. Hitherto, the first two sections, acting in concert, had easily out-voted the latter two which had remained mostly isolated from each other and had rarely combined their forces. Before the end of the year, however, a complete change took place. The Ministerial section gravitated rapidly towards the Free Traders, new combinations arose, and the boundaries of political parties had to be mapped out afresh.

Parliament was opened by the Queen on the 4th of February, in a speech the tone of which was cheerful and congratulatory. Trade had improved, the revenue had exceeded expectations, the harvest had been abundant, "private capital had been freely applied to useful public enterprises" (railways), and "the prospect of continued peace and the general state of domestic prosperity and tranquillity afford a favourable opportunity for," &c., &c. The Opposition abstained from moving an amendment to the Address, Lord John Russell contenting himself with making some incidental remarks, in the course of which he stated his conviction "that protection was not the support, but the bane of agriculture," to which Mr. Miles, naturally enough, replied by a question, "Why had Lord John Russell so persistently proposed a fixed duty on wheat if he was so convinced that protection was the bane of agriculture?"

The budget was brought forward this year at an unusually early period; it was on the 14th of February, only ten days after the opening of Parliament, that Sir Robert Peel set forth his financial plans in a committee of ways and means. In a most luminous speech that occupied upwards of three hours in the delivery, he gave a masterly exposition of the principles by which the incidence of taxation should be regulated, and also of the manner in which he had applied those principles in the present

1845. budget. We will briefly sum up the conclusions to which he arrived. He proposed—(1) to continue the income tax in order "to enable Parliament to repeal other taxes pressing on the industry and commercial enterprise of the country." This would give him a surplus of £3,400,000, which he intended to devote to the following purposes: (2) to reduce the sugar duties, as an article of general consumption among the poorer classes, by which reduction he calculated that the revenue would lose £1,300,000; (3) to repeal all duties on exports, including the £120,000 now derived from the export duty on coal; (4) to repeal the import duties on 430 out of the 813 articles now liable to such duties, which alteration would cost the revenue £320,000; (5) to repeal the import duty on raw cotton, which last year yielded £680,000; (6) to repeal the excise duty on glass, which last year yielded £642,000; and to effect some further fiscal reforms. The total revenue surrendered by these remissions amounted to £3,300,000.

This was essentially a Free-Trade budget as far as it went. True, it did not go far enough, but it went a long way in the right direction. The distance between extreme Protection and absolute Free Trade was too great to be cleared at one bound. The Free-Trade party might have accepted the present measure as an instalment, had they been assured that the remaining instalments would be punctually forthcoming. But no guarantees to that effect were offered by Sir Robert Peel, so that Cobden and his friends refused to give a receipt in full until the actual liquidation of the entire debt had been completed. The only serious opposition offered to the Ministerial budget was in reference to the sugar duties. On the 24th of February Mr. M. Gibson moved a resolution stating that "no arrangement of the sugar duties would be satisfactory and permanent which did not involve an equalisation of duty on foreign and colonial sugar." But this motion was negatived by a large majority, and Sir Robert Peel's financial measures passed without alteration or curtailment.

On the 13th of March Mr. Cobden moved for a select committee to inquire into the causes and extent of the alleged existing agricultural distress, and into the effect of legislative protection upon the interests of landowners, tenant-farmers, and farm-labourers." His speech on this occasion was one of the most effective that he ever delivered. Not only did it create a great sensation throughout the country, but it is said to have produced a deep impression on the mind of Sir Robert Peel himself. Towards its conclusion Mr. Cobden made a stirring appeal to the country gentlemen. "You are," he said, "the gentry of England who represent the counties. You are the aristocracy of England. Your fathers led our fathers; you may lead us if you go the right way. But although you have retained your influence with your country longer than any other aristocracy, it has not been by opposing popular opinion, or by setting yourselves against the spirit of the age. . . . This is a new era. It is the age of improvement, it is the age of social advancement, not the age for war or feudal sports. You live in a mercantile age when the whole wealth of world is poured into your

1845. lap. . . . The English people look to the gentry and aristocracy of their country as their leaders. I, who am not one of you, have no hesitation in telling you that there is a deep-rooted, a hereditary prejudice, if I may call it so, in your favour in this country. But you never got it, and you will not keep it, by obstructing the spirit of the age. If you are indifferent to enlightened means of finding employment for your own peasantry ; if you are found obstructing that advance which is calculated to knit nations more together in the bonds of peace by means of commercial intercourse ; if you are found fighting against the discoveries which have almost given breath and life to material nature, and setting yourselves up as obstructives of that which the community at large has decreed shall go on, why, then, you will be the gentry of England no longer, and others will be found to take your place."

The motion was opposed on behalf of Government by Sidney Herbert, the Secretary-at-War, in a somewhat indiscreet speech, in the course of which he said that "it was distasteful to him, as a member of the agricultural body, to be always coming to Parliament whining for protection." Mr. Cobden was denied his committee by a majority of ninety-two.

The landed interest, while mistrusting and repelling Cobden's proposition that their alleged grievances should be made the subject of inquiry, insisted clamorously on the existence of those grievances, and came forward themselves as claimants for public sympathy. On the 17th March Mr. Miles moved:—
" That it is the opinion of this House that in the

application of surplus revenue .... due regard should be had to the necessity of affording relief to the agricultural interests." His complaints were loud, and his demands small, but Sir J. Graham, on behalf of Government, opposed the motion, incidentally remarking that "with the rapid increase of our population many years would not pass away without the occurrence of some frightful convulsion if they were to persist in refusing admission to foreign corn." Mr. Newdegate echoed Mr. Miles' complaints. "He considered Mr. Cobden as the high-priest of Free Trade, and the occupants of the Treasury bench as fellow-worshippers who were chanting responses to the service which he performed."

A far more powerful voice now made itself heard, and the plaintive murmurs of the country gentlemen rose into stinging reproaches and incisive sarcasms in the mouth of Mr. B. Disraeli. After inveighing against the inconsistencies of the Prime Minister, and charging him with having deserted his party, he said: —"The right honourable baronet had once avowed that he was prouder of being leader of the country gentlemen of England than of being entrusted with the confidence of sovereigns. But where are the country gentlemen of England now? They are discovering the difference between the hours of courtship and the moments of possession; little is now said about them. When the beloved object has ceased to charm, it is useless to appeal to the feelings. Instead of listening to their complaints, the Premier sends down his valet, a well-behaved person, to make it known that we are to have no 'whining' here. (This allusion to Mr. S. Herbert's expression a few days before was received with vociferous cheering and loud laughter from the Opposition.) Such is the fate of the great agricultural interest—that beauty which everybody wooed and one deluded. . . . . Protection appears to be in about the same condition that Protestantism was in 1828. (Loud cheers from the Opposition.) The country will draw its moral. For my part, if we are to have Free Trade, I, who honour genius, prefer that such measures should be proposed by the honourable member for Stockport (Mr. Cobden) than by one who, though skilful in Parliamentary manœuvres, has tampered with the generous confidence of a great people and of a great party. For myself, I care not what will be the result. Dissolve, if you like, the Parliament you have betrayed, and appeal to the people who, I believe, mistrust you. For me, there remains this at least—the opportunity of expressing thus publicly my belief that a Conservative Government is an organised hypocrisy."

These taunts must have proved all the more galling to Sir Robert Peel from the vehement and long-continued cheering they elicited, not only from the Opposition, but also, in a marked degree, from the country party. Nor can we much wonder at this ebullition of feeling on the part of the agriculturists. Consider their position. It was their brawny shoulders that had borne Peel to the Premiership, for the express purpose—with, as they thought, the distinct understanding—and in the firm expectation, that the unseemly coquetry of the Whigs with Free Trade would be sternly repressed. But what did they find? They found that their leaders—Peel, Graham, and Gladstone—had themselves become deeply enamoured of that very object with which the Whigs had merely coquetted. The progress of Lord John Russell's administration towards a free commercial policy had been slow, feeble, and faltering. If upon such small provocation the country party had been roused to anger, we may imagine their horror at seeing their own trusted chiefs treading the same path, and with steadier step. It must be admitted that, from a party point of view, Mr. Disraeli's impeachment of the Premier seemed justified by the facts.

How far Sir Robert Peel was excusable in devoting the power he had acquired under certain tacit conditions to the attainment of aims utterly inconsistent with their fulfilment, is a question of political morality which we shall take another opportunity of discussing, but meanwhile we can easily conceive the mixed feelings of indignation and helplessness by which the country party was agitated. Indignation, because the course steered was exactly the opposite to that for which they had embarked; and helplessness, because if they dismissed the unfaithful steersman from the helm they could find no substitute, and would be left at the mercy of the winds, waves, and currents. Mr. Disraeli's strictures merely gave forcible expression to their bitterness and despair. Mr. Miles' motion was negatived by a large majority.

The agriculturists continued to contest the ground inch by inch, and somewhat compromised their dignity by raising debates on insignificant details. For instance, Mr. Bramston, member for South Essex,

1845. "objected to the removal of the duty on grease, as he dreaded that it would lead to a great importation of foreign butter." Sir G. Clerk endeavoured to quiet his fears by informing the House that whenever butter was imported under the name of grease it was immediately mixed with tar, so as to render it unfit for human food, and it was then used for smearing sheep. The House was consoled and comforted by this assurance that the use of foreign butter would be confined to sheep's backs, and would not reach human stomachs. A long discussion ensued. Some country members defended the remission of duty on grease, on the plea that in the north it was extensively used by sheep farmers. As Mr. Villiers remarked:—"Here was one county asking for protection against another. Here it was Northumberland against Essex; one had sheep to smear, the other grease to sell; and while the one asked admission for foreign grease, the other sought protection for the domestic article." Grease passed.

Next came another long debate on lard, which Mr. Grogan proposed to exclude from the list of remissions. Sir Robert Peel, weary of this trifling, threw out a broad hint that if grease and lard were to be thrown out of that list, butter and cheese might perhaps be inserted in their stead. Whereupon Mr. Cobden rose, and, addressing the agricultural members, cried—"Did we ever say anything so insulting to you as that? I have sometimes said at Covent Garden that there should be written over this House, 'Dealers in corn and cattle, and no competition allowed with the shop over the water.' But I never said that you were cheesemongers and dealers in butter. Is it not most degrading to you to say that the wretched serfs who earn eight or nine shillings a week must not purchase butter or cheese at a somewhat cheaper rate, because you are interested in keeping up the prices of these necessaries?" After that, lard passed. But the effect of such scenes was damaging to the Protectionists. They afforded matter for innumerable sarcastic remarks, telling caricatures, and satirical speeches, and W. J. Fox made them the subject of a most humorous and lively address at one of the Covent Garden Theatre meetings. A cause smitten by ridicule has received a deadly blow.

We must return for a while to the events passing outside of Parliament. A great national bazaar was to be held at Covent Garden Theatre, partly to swell the funds of the League, and partly for the reasons stated by Mr. G. Wilson, the chairman at a preparatory meeting on the 10th of April. "If money only were our object," he said, "a greater amount might easily be procured by a general subscription than we are likely to receive from this exhibition; but we want a more generally implied co-operation than the mere amount of money would imply. We want to see assembled in this theatre our friends from all parts of the kingdom in order that they may confer together; that they may become known to each other; that they may derive from such meetings, and from what they will see here, a new impetus, and carry to the extremities of the country a redoubled resolution to assist us in promoting the great object which we have in view."

The bazaar opened on the 8th of May, and proved

1845. eminently successful. Never before had Covent Garden Theatre presented so grand a spectacle. All the space that could be spared for the exhibition on stalls of articles for sale was crowded to excess with wares of every possible description, many of them of great beauty, rarity, and value, contributed by almost every town and district in the United Kingdom. They were classed and labelled according to the localities whence they came. So great was the variety, the excellence, and the value of many of the articles exhibited, that they very fairly illustrated the productive powers of the nation, and this not only far surpassed all similar collections hitherto known, but remained unsurpassed until eclipsed by the great Exhibition in Hyde Park, which, in 1851, Prince Albert devised and inaugurated, and for which Paxton built so fitting a temple.

The attendance, throughout the whole of the eighteen days that the bazaar lasted, was profuse, and it never slackened. From morning to night an unbroken stream of visitors filled every avenue. The total sum raised was £25,000, and there remained enough of unsold goods to furnish another bazaar that was held in the autumn at Manchester. The scene presented to a spectator from the galleries was most brilliant and animated. The vast profusion of various products of man's labour, the ever-shifting crowd of human beings, the splendid scenic decorations, the lights, the movement, the music, the subdued hum of voices, the associations connected with the origin and purpose of the spectacle, all combined to fill the mind of the beholder with varied and pleasing emotions.

Both the purposes which the League had in view were accomplished. Not only had its funds received a large addition, but the number of its adherents had also increased. Every buyer at the bazaar, if only of a shilling trifle, had by that act given his support to the League and its principles. He had, in a way, become identified with its career and acquired an interest in its success. He would henceforward sympathise with its struggles and finally participate in its triumph. But it was not its visitors alone that this great exhibition, the joint work of tens of thousands of contributors, impressed with admiration and wonder. There was not a newspaper or a serial publication, metropolitan or provincial, that was not full of the topic, which thus became the familiar talk of every household in the country. A felicitous idea had been worked out with skill and energy, and attended with complete success.

Lord John Russell moved, on the 26th of May, a string of resolutions relating to the condition of the working classes, and supported his motion by a speech of great ability. Of the eight resolutions which he put forward we shall give the second and third, as specially coming within the scope of the present work. They ran as follows:—"That those laws which impose duties, usually called protective, tend to impair the efficiency of labour, to restrict the free interchange of commodities, and to impose on the people unnecessary taxation;" and "That the present Corn Law tends to check improvements in agriculture, produces uncertainty in all farming speculations, and holds out to the owners and occupiers of land prospects of

1845. special advantage, which it fails to secure." These, it will be seen, amount to a clear declaration of complete Free-Trade principles; and the reasoning to which Lord John Russell resorted to to induce the House to pledge itself to such a declaration evinced the rapid advance which he had made, since his party had been in opposition, towards the doctrines of the Anti-Corn-Law League. In adverting to the policy of restriction and monopoly, or as it was sometimes called, the policy of protection to native industry, he proclaimed the necessity of "altogether overturning that erroneous system." He had convinced himself "that the policy of restriction was mischievous, that it favoured one class at the expense of another, and that it injured the labouring classes more than any other." He contended that the agricultural interests were not benefited by the present Corn Law, "for it appeared that now, when they had a protection of 40 per cent. on the ordinary food of the people, they were still in a state of difficulty and distress." He did not, it is true, go so far as to advocate the complete removal of all duties on corn; but he declared that he would not renew his proposition for an 8s. duty, and it was in so feeble and lukewarm a tone that he suggested some low fixed duty that no one could doubt his readiness to yield, under very slight additional pressure, to the full measure of total repeal. "Now is the time," he said, "to enfranchise trade and industry—now, with political tranquillity and leisure, with bread at Free-Trade prices, with revived commerce and prosperous manufactures — now, with population growing at an almost fearful rate of increase—now, before another bad harvest brings on the cry of hunger."

Sir James Graham and Sir R. Peel opposed the motion on general grounds, and without expressing dissent from the commercial policy advocated by the mover. Indeed, alluding to a statement made by Sir John Tyrrell, that Government had forfeited the confidence of the agricultural interest, Sir Robert Peel said, in the most outspoken manner, that he did not know whether Sir John Tyrrell was authorised to speak as the organ of that interest; but even if he were, he (Sir R. Peel) "would not purchase back again the confidence which he was said to have forfeited by uttering the slightest expression of repentance for the course which he had pursued." The previous question (the politest form of refusal) was moved by Sir James Graham, and carried by a majority of 78.

The time had now come round for the annual motion on the Corn Law, which Mr. Villiers had for so many years brought forward with unfaltering persistency. He had assumed the parliamentary guardianship of Free-Trade principles at a time when they were neglected, misunderstood, and unpopular. Gradually he had seen public opinion, instructed and guided by men of great talent and energy, swerve round to them, and their truth recognised by numerous converts, not only among the rank and file of Englishmen, but also among the foremost group of English statesmen. Now, in 1845, he was about to submit his proposition to the suffrages of an assembly, of which the majority, he knew beforehand,

1845. assented to his theoretical views, but would nevertheless refuse their assent to his motion. He was consoled by the reflection, that though the opposition to it was to all appearance real, in reality it was a sham. Many would vote against him whose convictions were with him, and he felt sure that the time would come when the convictions would remain, and it would be the votes that would change.

It was on the 10th of June that Mr. Villiers moved for a committee of the whole House, for the purpose of considering the following resolutions:— 1. "That the Corn Law restricts the supply of food and prevents the free exchange of the products of labour. 2. That it is, therefore, prejudicial to the welfare of the country, especially to that of the working classes, and has proved delusive to those for whose benefit the law was designed. 3. That it is expedient that all restrictions on (foreign) corn should be now abolished." The debate elicited no new feature, for by this time every argument pro and con had been exhausted, and every topic worn threadbare. Mr. Villiers concluded by saying that if the agriculturists could show that they bore special and exceptional burdens, let them send in their bill, and let Government meet it in any way they pleased, except that of making the food of the people dear.

Sir James Graham would not deny that it was his opinion that, by a gradual and cautious policy, it was expedient to bring our system of Corn Laws into a nearer approximation to those wholesome principles which now govern our legislation with respect to other industrial departments; but he was utterly opposed to the sudden change demanded by Mr. Villiers. Mr. Bright knew that when they went to a division they would be in a minority; but minorities in that House had often become majorities, and he hoped to see that result produced again. Mr. G. Bankes considered it " very unfair in the manufacturers to attempt to take away from the landowners the protection which they had enjoyed for many years." Mr. Cobden, in answer to the charge of rashness brought against the League, asked whether there was ever such rashness as to leave 27,000,000 of people with a stock of only 300,000 quarters of foreign wheat to stand between them and famine in case of another bad harvest? Lord John Russell said that he "saw the fall of the Corn Law signified not only by the ability of the attacks made upon it, but also by the manner in which it is defended in this House." Sir Robert Peel insisted on the necessity for prudence and caution, and could not consent to a proposition "that implied the total disregard of such considerations in the application of the principle of Free Trade." The motion was negatived by 254 votes against 122.

CHAPTER XI.
(1845.)

The League's £100,000 Fund raised—Bad Weather in September injures the English Harvest—First appearance in Ireland of the Potato Disease—Perplexity and Indecision of Ministers—Dissensions in the Cabinet—Sir Robert Peel Resigns—Lord John Russell unable to form a Ministry—Return to Power of Sir Robert Peel—Remarks on his Position—The League proposes to raise a Fund of £250,000.

1845. THE League held one of its great meetings at Covent Garden Theatre on the 18th of June. The chairman, Mr. George Wilson, announced that the contributions to the £100,000 fund now amounted, including the sum realised from the late bazaar, to more than £116,000. Mr. Cobden in his speech observed that "they had now brought the adoption of Free Trade to a mere question of time. They had narrowed it down to one little word—When? That question he answered in another little word—Now!" Mr. Bright also made a brilliant speech, in which he said, adverting to Sir Robert Peel: "From his recent speech, I would argue that he intends to repeal the Corn Laws. He cannot say what he does and yet mean to go back to the old foolish policy of Protection. . . . He sprung from commerce, and until he has proved it himself, I will never believe that there is any man, much less will I believe that he is the man, who would go down to his grave, having had the power to deliver that commerce, and yet not having the manliness, honesty, and courage to do it." Mr. W. J. Fox alluded in a similar strain of hope and exultation to the progress which Sir Robert Peel and his colleagues were making towards a policy of commercial freedom. The theory was not only freely conceded by them, but openly proclaimed. The only difference of opinion was as to how soon theory should be concreted into practice.

This adoption of Free-Trade principles was not the result of pressure from adverse circumstances. The country was flourishing, trade was prosperous, the revenue showed a surplus, railways were being constructed with unexampled rapidity, the working classes were fully and remuneratively employed, the imperial average of wheat for the week ending June 28th was 47s. 11d. per quarter, and bread was cheaper than it had been for many years. The prevailing convergence towards Free-Trade principles simply proceeded from a conscientious recognition of economic truths. It was felt that the continuance of the existing prosperity could not be ensured unless our commercial policy were conducted in conformity with scientific principles.

On the 5th of August Lord John Russell, in reviewing the session about to close, alluded to the unsettled weather which had recently prevailed, and to the apprehensions that had arisen as to its effect on the growing crops. The next fortnight's weather might prove decisive, and under that uncertainty who would not "wish that the labouring classes should be provided with food from all quarters where it can be obtained? I maintain that it is the duty of this House to provide for such a contingency." But Lord John Russell spoke in vain, and on the 9th Parliament was prorogued.

The state of the weather and the prospects of the wheat crop were now watched with intense anxiety.

1845. By the middle of August the price of wheat had risen to 57s. per quarter. But a few occasional fine days in the early part of September excited hopes that the harvest, though late, might still approach to an average, and in the second week in September the price fell to 54s. Towards the end of the month, however, it became manifest that the crop would be far below an average, in quality as well as in quantity. Markets became excited, and a rise took place of several shillings per quarter. The impending disaster threatened a relapse into that dearness and scarcity from which England had suffered so much a few years before.

But that misfortune sank into comparative insignificance in the face of the far more dreadful calamity which exposed millions of our Irish fellow-subjects to all the horrors of absolute famine. Nearly the entire food-supply relied on to maintain three-fourths of the population of Ireland was suddenly, unexpectedly, and irretrievably annihilated. A pestilential blight, never known or heard of till that fatal year, had smitten the potato plant, and rendered its tubers utterly unfit for human food. Its easy culture, requiring little labour and little capital, and the large returns which it usually yielded, had allured the people into devoting nearly the whole of their land to its cultivation. Time was when Ireland had raised wheat and oats in excess of her own consumption, and had exported to England considerable quantities of grain and flour. But by degrees corn-fields had merged into potato-fields. The simple process of planting, digging up, and pitting potatoes, required so little labour and occupied so little time, as compared with the toilsome and multifarious processes connected with cereal-growing, that the easy-going and light-hearted Irish peasant felt irresistibly attracted to the former.

Unfortunately, there lurked behind this fatal facility of production a fearful danger, the extent of which even William Cobbett, the bitter reviler of what he called the "pauperising root," could not have foreseen. That the produce was variable and, as a source of national wealth, unprofitable, was well known, but no one had contemplated the possibility of the entire crop throughout the land being swept away by disease within a few weeks. Such a catastrophe had, however, now occurred. Such portion of the crop as had been apparently sound when dug up, became a putrid mass shortly after being pitted. The result was a great fall for a time in the price, for all the potatoes that seemed externally free from disease were hurried to market and sold for whatever they might fetch.

It was, of course, not Ireland alone that was subjected to this visitation; it extended to Great Britain, Belgium, and many parts of the continent of Europe. But while the disease was more widespread and intense, and its ravages more destructive, in Ireland than elsewhere, Ireland was at the same time the only country in the world in which potatoes were the staple, and in many districts the only, food of the people. Elsewhere that esculent was cultivated to a limited extent, and formed quite a subordinate crop. In Ireland it was not only the main, but in many cases the sole, produce of the land.

1845. In the face of this overwhelming calamity any further resistance by Government to the demands of the Free Traders seemed hopeless. The bad English harvest alone would have sufficed to hasten the approaching repeal of the Corn Law, but that the repeal must now be near at hand soon became evident. Class interests, party politics, personal considerations—all would have to give way in the face of one terrible fact—the impending starvation of the Irish people. Sir Robert Peel and some of his colleagues were fully alive to the importance of the crisis. Dr. Lyon Playfair and Professor Lindley were dispatched to Ireland to examine and report on the nature and extent of the evil. They confirmed the worst accounts that had been received.

By the 15th of October Sir Robert Peel began to contemplate the probable necessity of resorting to extreme measures. He wrote on that day to Sir James Graham as follows: "My letter on the awful state of the potato crop in Ireland crossed yours to me. . . . Interference with the due course of the laws respecting the supply of food is so momentous and so lasting in its consequences, that we must not act without the most accurate information. I fear the worst." He well knew that a temporary removal of the import duty on foreign corn meant a permanent repeal; and that the step, once taken, would be "lasting in its consequences," and could never be retraced. What it was so difficult to retain would never, if parted with, be recovered. The "accurate information" which he sought was received, but it only painted the picture in darker colours; and his "fears of the worst" were day by day being realised.

Meanwhile the country was impatiently looking to Ministers to take some decided steps to meet the coming emergency, and murmured at their apparent inaction. It was, however, not neglect, but indecision, which delayed the action of Government. Ministers were overpoweringly conscious of the responsibility thrown upon them, but could not agree as to the course which should be adopted. Sir Robert Peel advocated bold and prompt measures, but was supported by a part only of his colleagues. A Cabinet Council was held on the 31st of October, at which these dissensions were strongly manifested. It separated without coming to any decision, and adjourned to the 6th of November. On that day the Cabinet met, and Sir Robert Peel formally submitted to Ministers for their adoption the following programme :—1. To issue immediately an Order in Council, reducing the duty on grain in bond to one shilling per quarter. 2. To open the ports to the temporary admission of all grain at a small rate of duty. 3. To call Parliament together on the 27th of November to ask for an indemnity, and to announce the intention of submitting immediately after the recess a modification of the existing Corn Laws. These propositions met with the support of only three of the Prime Minister's colleagues—Sir James Graham, the Earl of Aberdeen, and Mr. Sidney Herbert—and, accordingly, the deliberations led to no practical issue.

 Among the public the excitement was intense. The country felt itself on the eve of great changes. Free Trade had long been wished for, worked for, waited for; now it seemed close at hand. In what

1845. shape would it come? The uncertainty was tantalising. The corn trade was in a state of suspense and consequent confusion. Large and regular importations of corn would require previous preparation, organisation, and freight arrangements, which no prudent man would enter upon till he knew the conditions on which foreign corn would be admitted. Men felt aggrieved at being left in the dark, but still Ministers gave no sign.

A meeting of the League was held in the Manchester Free Trade Hall on the 28th of October. Eight thousand persons obtained admittance, while numbers were turned away. Richard Cobden and John Bright were the chief speakers. Mr. Cobden pointed out that the obvious remedy for the fearful evils with which we were threatened was to throw open our ports. No half measures should be sanctioned, but a full measure of relief should be insisted on. Mr. Bright followed in a short but animated speech, in the course of which he observed: "It has been said that the Corn Law was a law to secure plenty. Where, then, in this hour of apprehended scarcity, of distrust and alarm, should we so readily turn in the hope of relief, as to this very Corn Law?" He then proceeded to show that it aggravated, not relieved, our wants, and added, "Peel's pet law is now working precisely as its supporters wished it to work. It was to prevent the trade in corn—to make you and your fellow workmen work and work, and scramble and scramble, and starve, it may be, in order that out of the produce of your industry, out of the scanty wages of the many, something may be taken by law, and handed over to the rich, by whom the law was made." Numerous other meetings were held in different parts of the country, at all of which a resolution was passed to memorialise the Government instantly to open the ports.

In the midst of this excitement, Lord John Russell addressed, under date of the 22nd of November, a public letter to the electors of the City of London, in which he announces the solemn renunciation of his favourite old crotchet of a fixed duty on corn. After blaming the Ministers for having met and separated without affording any promise of seasonable relief, he confesses that "on the general subject my views have, in the course of twenty years, undergone a great alteration. .... It is no longer worth while to contend for a fixed duty. .. The imposition of any duty, at present, without a provision for its speedy extinction, would only prolong a contest already sufficiently fruitful of animosity and discontent." The Free-Trade party construed this letter as Dr. Johnson did Lord Chesterfield's tardy patronage after he had completed his task, and did not very highly value the co-operation of one who only ceased to oppose them when they had consummated their triumph, and who then "encumbered them with his help."

The three last weeks in November were busily employed by Sir Robert Peel and his colleagues in proposing, opposing, trimming, and compounding among themselves, so as to arrive, if possible, at some average scheme which would meet with the approval of the entire Cabinet—a difficult, not to say hopeless, task. With every desire to pull together, no one of them could help pulling a little too much his own way to satisfy the rest. A letter was drafted to the Lord Lieutenant of Ireland which described the peril that was impending in vigorous and graphic language. This was unanimously approved of, for it was the remedies, not the facts, about which they disagreed. But then came Sir Robert Peel's remark that it was "difficult to reconcile the issue of this letter with passiveness and inaction in respect to the means of increasing the supply of food." As a natural sequence to this objection he notified to his colleagues that he could not "consent to its issue, and undertake at the same time to maintain the existing Corn Laws."

On the 29th of November he addressed a note to the Duke of Wellington, giving the reasons which induced him to advise "the suspension of the existing Corn Laws for a limited period!" This memorandum was also communicated to the other Ministers. The Duke, in his bluff, honest, practical way, did not stay to discuss the abstract principle, but went straight to the question of feasibility. In his reply, he substantially says: "Do not let us break up the Corn Law unless there be an absolute necessity for it; but if there be, let us do so without hesitation. Consider, however, whether Sir Robert Peel could carry on the Queen's Government if the support of the landed interest were withdrawn from him. In respect to my own course, my only object is to support Sir Robert Peel's administration of the Queen's Government. . . . I earnestly recommend that the Cabinet should support him, and I for one declare that I will do so."

But the matter presented itself in a more complex form to the minds of the other members of the Cabinet, and several of them differed from the view taken by the single-minded soldier. They were swayed to and fro by a variety of conflicting considerations, and, finding a host of objections to every conclusion, came to none. This state of things could not last, and to put an end to it, Sir Robert Peel on the 2nd December proposed to his colleagues a specific proposal for a new law, "founded on the principles of the present law, while it continues in operation, but which will, in the course of that operation, ensure the ultimate and not remote extinction of protective duties." But the project met with no warm support, and both Lord Stanley and the Duke of Buccleugh declined assenting to any measure involving the ultimate repeal of the Corn Laws.

On the morning of the 4th December the country was startled by an announcement in the *Times* that Government had determined to repeal the Corn Laws and to call Parliament together in January for that purpose. The *Standard* of the 5th characterised this as an " atrocious fabrication." But the *Times* of the 6th reiterated its assertion, and another contemporary journal stated that "the effect of the announcement by the *Times* at the Corn Exchange was immense surprise—not so much displeasure as might have been expected—and an instant downward tendency in the price of grain." How the *Times* obtained its information was never known, but it was substantially correct so far as being the policy of a powerful section of the Cabinet. As, however, unanimity was unattain-

1845. able, Sir Robert Peel considered it his duty to resign, and on the 5th December he proceeded to Osborne, and humbly solicited the Queen "to relieve him from duties which he could no longer discharge with advantage to her Majesty's service."

Lord John Russell, who at the moment was in Edinburgh, was summoned to attend the Queen. He reached Osborne on the 11th. He had almost predetermined to decline the premiership. He entertained anxious misgivings as to the propriety of undertaking to form an administration while his party was in a minority of nearly 100 in the House of Commons, and as to a general election at a crisis so momentous, no prudent statesman could venture to recommend it. Lord John Russell's difficulties and scruples were however met by the Queen's placing in his hands a letter which Sir Robert Peel had, with that view, addressed to her on the 8th. In that letter he offered to support, in a private capacity, measures for the settlement of the Corn-Law question, on the basis of a gradual diminution and ultimate removal of duties on foreign grain, and to exercise any influence he might possess to promote the success of such measures. This assurance of support, which he vainly endeavoured to obtain in a less general and more definite form, finally induced Lord John Russell, on consultation with his friends, to accept the honourable task assigned to him. Accordingly, on the 18th of December, he informed her Majesty that he was ready to undertake the formation of a government. On the 19th Sir Robert Peel was invited by the Queen to a parting interview the next day, on the occasion of the severance of their political relations. But an unforeseen incident gave a new turn to affairs. Lord John Russell had counted on his Cabinet combining the powerful co-operation of Lord Grey and Lord Palmerston. The talents and influence of both were essential to its vitality. But at the last moment, Lord Grey, who had always disapproved of the warlike tendencies of Lord Palmerston's foreign policy, definitively refused to form part of a Ministry in which that statesman was to have the direction of foreign affairs. This discordance and incompatibility between two of the leading members of the embryo administration decided its fate. Lord John Russell, half disgusted, half relieved, relinquished his functions in despair. On the morning of the 20th the Queen received a letter from him stating that he had found it impossible to form an administration, and which concluded by saying that "he must now consider that task as hopeless which has been from the beginning hazardous." He simultaneously gave the same intimation to Sir Robert Peel.

When, on that day, the latter presented himself to the Queen at Windsor Castle, she, in her most gracious manner, said to him, "So far from taking leave of you, Sir Robert, I must require you to withdraw your resignation and to remain in my service." Sir Robert Peel, not unprepared for the contingency, signified his readiness to obey her Majesty's commands, and he returned to town once more Prime Minister of England. All his old colleagues rallied round him save two—Lord Stanley, who could not see

1845. why going out and coming in again should alter his convictions, and Lord Wharncliffe who had meanwhile died. They were replaced by two men who brought a great accession of strength to the Ministry, Mr. W. E. Gladstone and Lord Dalhousie.

Sir Robert Peel's retirement from, so quickly followed by his restoration to, power, had the effect of greatly increasing his individual authority, and as a consequence, of proportionately increasing his individual responsibility. Before his resignation his colleagues had full power to suggest, modify, object, or even reject; but after their resumption of office under peculiar circumstances, they merged their political identity into his, and there was a clear though tacit understanding that the forthcoming measures and policy were to be shaped by him. This responsibility Peel readily adopted and boldly exercised amid a storm of obloquy and personal invective from some, and the ungracious approval and somewhat sarcastic applause of others. He was assailed on two grounds—1, that he had changed his opinions on the subject of Free Trade *versus* Protection; 2, that having changed those opinions, he had not resigned the leadership of the Conservative party.

To the charge of having changed his opinion on a debatable question of political economy, the answer is obvious. If that change was the result of earnest inquiry and of conscientious conviction, it was not only not reprehensible, but it was highly praiseworthy. Adherence to detected error is only another form of apostasy from acknowledged truth. That Peel did not, at an earlier period in life, perceive the error or ascertain the truth, may be a reproach to his intellect, but cannot be a stain upon his character. Where is the man whom the experience of a life has left unaltered in all his youthful opinions? If there be such men, they must be commonplace persons, unobservant and unreasoning, who, having caught, like burs, at the prevailing notion of their day, have got entangled and fixed there. They are consistent (as it is called) simply because they are unchanged; and they are unchanged because they are mentally purblind. The man who, having reached the age of fifty, retains the precise opinions which he held at the age of twenty, must either have had the exceptional good fortune of hitting, at that early period of life, upon the exact, complete, and irrefragable truth on all subjects, or he must have shut his eyes and ears to the reception of the new facts, new ideas, and new arguments which the progress of human inquiry are constantly bringing before us. Peel's convictions were perfectly sincere at every stage of their transfer from one to another set of opinions. His gradual conversion to, his subsequent open recognition of, and his final resolve to act upon, the principles of Free Trade, were operations inspired by the dictates of conscience—certainly not by the promptings of self-interest. Who, therefore, shall cast blame upon him in this respect, unless it be the "superior person"—that "faultless monster"— who, being infallible himself, exacts from others the same absolute perfection, susceptible of neither progress nor improvement?

But he retained, it may be said, the leadership

1845. of the Conservative party. Why should he not? Conservatism, as a system, embraced a large number of distinctive and important principles, of which "Protection" was only one, and a very subordinate one. To make our commercial policy the Shibboleth of the party was to rest its existence on the narrowest possible basis. Quite recently we have lived under a government decidedly Conservative, by which Free-Trade principles were openly advocated, and a retrograde policy steadily resisted. To have consigned the Conservative party to disruption on account of dissidences on so minor a point as the question of Customs duties, would have been inexcusable. Indeed, the party, as a whole, evidently took that view. Both before and when Peel took office in 1841, he plainly declared his belief that a restrictive policy would have to be gradually abandoned. He gave timely and repeated warnings. When Mr. Miles and his friends put him in a minority on the sugar question in 1844, he emphatically placed before his party the alternative of either accepting his resignation and constructing a fresh Ministry based on their own views, or of rescinding their vote and leaving him to follow up his own policy. He refused either to be hurried in his course by the Free-Trade party, or to be stopped in his advance by the Protectionists.

The landlords who, after all, only formed a cohort of the Conservative legion, found themselves powerless, and abandoned the struggle. Sir Robert Peel naturally inferred that their submission implied, if not a sanction, at least a reluctant assent, to his views, and that he was then at liberty to pursue the policy which he had announced. His intention was to introduce his Free-Trade measures in such gradations as would inflict the smallest possible disturbance on existing interests, but a portentous calamity precipitated his action. Again he encountered resistance, this time in the Cabinet, and he resigned. But no "possible man" could be found to replace him, and he resumed office under circumstances which made the adoption of his programme a foregone conclusion.

In what respect was his conduct blameworthy? Twice he gave the landlord party an opportunity of supplanting him. They proved utterly unequal to the task. He volunteered his support in a private capacity to Lord John Russell to carry through the measures which his own colleagues had refused to sanction. Lord John Russell failed to form an administration. What was Sir Robert Peel to do? Was he then to dismember and disorganise the great Conservative party by persistently abdicating its leadership? No doubt there was a middle course. He might have retained his convictions and acted in opposition to them. He might for a brief period (and for a very brief period) have stemmed the torrent of public opinion. He might, at the expense of his conscience, and at the risk of plunging his country into confusion, have remained the idolised chief of a party.

But Sir Robert Peel was not the man to adopt so unworthy a course. He preferred the noble ambition of doing good to the ignoble ambition of being great. There was the impending Irish famine to meet. On

1845. him had devolved that grave task. It was a duty from which he must not shrink, though he saw that its performance, while it profited him nothing, would cost him dear. For, indeed, what could he possibly gain? He had reached the acme of political eminence. He was the virtual ruler of England, and, as far as the power and influence of England would warrant it, he was the arbiter of the world. On the other hand, what would it cost him? Nothing less than the friendship of old friends, the support of old supporters, the admiration of old admirers, and the confidence of those who had trusted him. What would it entail upon him? The loss of his political *prestige*, the enmity of a great party, the cold, averted looks of former friends, the bitter taunts of those who suffered, or thought they suffered, from his desertion; obloquy, sneers, satire, and sarcastic invectives.

Could such a man, in such a position, with so much to lose and so little to gain, be otherwise actuated than by the profoundest sense of duty? Since his death, justice, and barely justice, has been done to his memory; but posterity will adjudge to him the superlative merit of having made greater sacrifices to truth and conscience than any other English statesman that ever lived.

The return of Sir Robert Peel to power, with the prospect that he would use it to pass Free-Trade measures, did not lull the Anti-Corn-Law League into inaction. On the contrary, they felt that they could support his measures with all the greater efficiency, if they increased their strength and displayed unabated vigour. Accordingly, they held a meeting in the

Manchester Town Hall on the 23rd December, Mr. R. H. Greg in the chair. The first business was to receive a report from Mr. G. Wilson, showing that the total amount raised by the last subscription was £123,000, of which £60,000 was expended in 1844, and £51,000 in 1845, leaving a balance in hand of £12,000. A resolution was passed that " a subscription, in aid of the great fund of £250,000, be now commenced." The chairman called on the assemblage to back their words by their deeds, and he set the example by subscribing £1,000. A rush of subscriptions then poured in, and in an hour and a half, at a single meeting, upwards of £60,000 was subscribed.

A few days afterwards a large meeting was held in the Free Trade Hall, which was so crowded that seats were removed from the body of the hall to increase the accommodation, and thus the usual 8,000 auditors became 9,000 on this occasion. Reports were received of the additional subscriptions that had, since the first meeting, flowed in from various towns and districts throughout the country, and the total already amounted to £150,000. It should be borne in mind—for it is truly noteworthy—that this magnificent sum was raised in a few weeks, for a patriotic purpose, by contributions that were purely voluntary. A rare display of unstinted liberality and of deep devotion to a cause!

CHAPTER XII.
(1846.)

Sir Robert Peel's bold and comprehensive Financial Measures—The remaining Import Duties again largely Reduced—Total Repeal of the Corn Laws to take place in 1849, with, meanwhile, only a moderate Import Duty—Interesting Debates—Ministerial Triumph—Irish Coercion Bill—Ministerial Defeat—Resignation of Sir Robert Peel.

1846. THE Session of 1846 was opened on the 19th of January, by the Queen in person. In her speech reference was made to the failure of the potato crop in Ireland, and to measures for "enlarging our commercial intercourse." But on this occasion, the debate on the address was chiefly confined to explanations from Sir Robert Peel and Lord John Russell, on the Ministerial negotiations. In his speech, Sir Robert Peel adverted to the potato famine, as having given more immediate urgency to the Corn Law question, adding, " I will not assign to that cause too much weight. I will not withhold the homage which is due to the progress of reason and truth, by denying that my opinions on the subject of Protection have undergone a change. . . . It may be supposed that there is something humiliating in making such admissions; I feel no such humiliation. . . . I should feel humiliated if, having modified or changed my opinion, I declined to acknowledge the change, for fear of incurring the imputation of inconsistency." He concluded a long and able speech, which was much cheered, especially by the Opposition, by these words : " I do not desire to be the Minister of England ; but while I am Minister of England I will hold office by no servile tenure—I will hold office unshackled by any other obligation than that of consulting the public interests, and providing for the public safety."

It was evident that he had not lost his hold over the majority of the House; but that it was their votes, and not their hearts, that went with him, was equally evident, from the vociferous cheers that greeted the vehement onslaught made upon him by Mr. Disraeli, who with Lord George Bentinck, led the small band of Irreconcileables. One of the points in his cutting speech that elicited the most applause was his comparison of the Prime Minister to the Turkish High Admiral, who had handed over the Sultan's fleet to the rebel Pasha of Egypt. "Now," said Mr. Disraeli, "the Lord High Admiral was very much misrepresented. He, too, was called traitor, and he too vindicated himself. 'True it is,' said he, 'I did place myself at the head of this noble armament—true it is that my sovereign embraced me,—true it is that all the muftis in the empire offered up prayers for my success; but I have an objection to war. I see no use in prolonging the struggle; and the only reason I had for accepting the command was that I might terminate the contest by betraying my master." The House laughed and applauded, but showed no symptom of resistance, and the address was adopted without a division.

On the 27th of January, Sir Robert Peel, in a most lucid and comprehensive speech, which occupied four hours in the delivery, developed his plan of financial and commercial policy. The House was crowded, and

1846. every available space for visitors was thronged with eager listeners, among whom were Prince Albert and the Duke of Cambridge. He called not only on the agriculturists but on every protected class to relinquish Protection. The principal changes which he proposed were as follows:—All duties on foreign manufactured goods were to be abolished, or greatly reduced; abolished on the coarser descriptions, reduced from 20 per cent. to 10 per cent. on the finer qualities. Duties on timber and tallow, the only two articles of raw material on which they remained unrepealed, were reduced more than one-half. Silk goods were to be admitted at 15 per cent. duty instead of 30 per cent. The differential duties on free-labour sugar were reduced by one-half. Animal food and vegetables were admitted duty free, as also maize and buckwheat. One-half of the existing duties on butter, cheese, hops, and cured fish were removed. In short, the duties were to be reduced, or altogether repealed, on more than 150 articles. Finally, as to wheat, oats, barley, and rye, he proposed that on the 1st of February, 1849 (in three years), they should be admitted duty free, subject only to a small nominal registration tax; in other words, he proposed the TOTAL REPEAL OF THE CORN LAWS. It was to take place in three years, and meanwhile the duties to be levied on wheat were reduced to 10s. per quarter when the price was under 48s. per quarter. At every rise of one shilling per quarter in the market price the duty was to be one shilling per quarter lower, till wheat should be at 54s., and the duty at 4s., after which the duty was not further to change. The existing price of wheat being

54s., the duty would be at once reduced from 16s. to 4s. per quarter.

In conclusion, Sir Robert Peel said :—" I ask you to give your consent to this measure, not upon any narrow view that its principle is connected with the accumulation of wealth. . . . The true source of increased revenue is the increased comfort and the unseen voluntary taxation which arises from increased consumption. I ask you to give your consent, upon proof advanced to you that abundance and cheapness lead to diminished crime and increased morality." It was then arranged that the House should enter on the discussion of Sir Robert Peel's resolutions on the 9th of February.

Accordingly, on that evening a debate commenced on an amendment, moved by Mr. Miles, to go into Committee "that day six months." The debate lasted twelve nights. Speeches were delivered to the number of 103, of which 48 were in favour of Free Trade, and 55 on the side of Protection. The patient and laborious drudge who has waded through these finds in them mostly a mass of verbiage, consisting of the dull repetition, in a slightly-varied form, of the old, stale arguments on either side, illumined, however, by a few bright flashes of eloquence, and occasionally enlivened by a smart hit or a telling point. To a few of these we may be permitted to refer.

Lord John Russell, who was the first member of the Opposition who had risen, announced, amid cheers, his intention of voting with the Ministers. He recommended immediate repeal in preference to any delay. "But," added he, "I wish the plan of the right

1846. honourable gentleman to succeed. . . . If therefore when we come into Committee, he tells me that, upon the whole, he considers the delay of three years, and the duty to be imposed in the meantime, an essential part of his plan, I, for my part, shall go out with the right honourable gentleman upon it. . . . If he has the glory of carrying a measure fraught with such large and beneficial results, let ours be the solid satisfaction that out of office we have associated for the purpose of aiding and assisting the triumph of the Minister of the Crown." Mr. T. Baring thought the want in Ireland greatly exaggerated. He believed that the greatest want under which the country laboured was the want of Ministers, and the most appalling scarcity was that of statesmen who would consent to sit together in the same Cabinet. . . He could see no justification of the sweeping change now proposed. Mr. W. Miles accused Sir Robert Peel of throwing overboard all the industrial energies of the country, and leaving us to compete under our heavy taxation, with the untaxed energies of Germany and the United States. . . He foresaw that the time would soon arrive when the people of these Islands would curse the day when first their government was entrusted to a temporising Free-Trade Minister.

Sir Robert Peel, who spoke on the sixth night of the debate, concluded a long and powerful speech by the following eloquent peroration. "This night is to decide between the policy of continued relaxation of restriction, or the return to restraint and prohibition. This night you will select the motto, which is to indicate the commercial policy of England. Shall it be advance or recede? Which is the fitter motto for this great empire? Survey our position; consider the advantages which God and nature have given us, and the destiny for which we are intended. We stand on the confines of Western Europe, the chief connecting-link between the old world and the new. The discoveries of science, the improvements in navigation, have brought us within ten days of St. Petersburg, and will soon bring us within ten days of New York. We have an extent of coast greater, in proportion to our population and the area of our land, than any other great nation, securing to us maritime strength and superiority. Iron and coal, the sinews of manufacture, give us advantages over every rival in the great competition of industry. Our capital far exceeds that which they can command. In ingenuity, in skill, in energy, we are inferior to none. Our national character, the free institutions under which we live, the liberty of thought and action, an unshackled press spreading the knowledge of every discovery and of every advance in science, combine with our natural and physical advantages to place us at the head of those nations which profit by the free interchange of their products. And is this the country to shrink from competition? Is this the country to adopt a retrograde policy? Is this the country which can only flourish in the sickly atmosphere of prohibition? Is this the country to stand shivering on the brink of exposure to the healthful breezes of competition?" So much for the general question of Free Trade; then addressing the agriculturists in particular, he exclaimed, "When the years of dearth may have come. . . when

1846. you are exhorting a suffering people to fortitude under their privations... and encouraging them to bear without repining the dispensations of Providence, may God grant that by your decision of this night you may have laid in store for yourselves the consolation of reflecting that such calamities are, in truth, the dispensations of Providence,—that they have not been caused, they have not been aggravated, by the laws of man restricting in the hours of scarcity the supply of food!"—Noble ideas clothed in noble words!

The next evening Mr. John Bright delivered a brilliant speech, which embodied a generous and glowing defence of Sir Robert Peel. "I watched the right honourable baronet go home last night," he said, "and I confess I envied him the ennobling feelings which must have filled his breast after delivering his speech—a speech, I venture to say, more powerful and more to be admired than any speech ever heard in this House, within the memory of any man in it. .... There is not," he continued, addressing himself to the Protectionist party, "a man in your ranks who would dare to sit on that bench as the Prime Minister of England, pledged to maintain the existing law. .... When the right honourable baronet resigned, he was then no longer your Minister. He came back to office as the Minister of his Sovereign and of the people—and not again as the Minister of a class who had made him such for their own selfish objects." It is said that tears were observed to start from the eyes of Sir Robert, usually so impassive, at this genial eulogy on the part of a high-minded adversary. It is by such sympathies that great souls comprehend and draw towards each other.

Richard Cobden maintained that an appeal to the country would yield a majority adverse to the Protectionist party. True, they might have their pocket boroughs and their nomination counties, but every town numbering more than 20,000 inhabitants would be against them. He wound up by saying, "We have set an example to the world in all ages. We have given the world the example of a free Press—of a representative Government—of civil and religious liberty—and we are going, I trust, to give them an example more glorious than all—that of making industry free, and of giving it the advantage of every clime and every latitude under Heaven."

Lord G. Bentinck contributed some bold statements. He contended that the working classes would be better off with undiminished wages and wheat at 70s. per quarter, than with corn at 45s. and reduced means of procuring it. The apprehension of impending famine was altogether a mistake. The crop was more than an average one. . . . The potato murrain was by no means so ex ensive as it had been represented. . . . . Half the evil was attributable to the conduct of Government in sending Commissioners to Ireland and creating an alarm. The potatoes were dug up before they were ripe, and they rotted." It is doubtful whether all the oratory which 103 speakers contributed to the twelve nights' debate converted a single hearer, or influenced a single vote, but it nevertheless fulfilled a requirement. It afforded to the country an exhaustive view of all that could be advanced on either side, and made patent to the world in the present and in the future, that the policy adopted was not the result of hasty or incomplete deliberation. On the division the numbers were: for Mr. Miles's amendment, 240; against it, 337; being a majority for the Government of 97.

On the 2nd of March the House went into Committee, on which occasion Mr. Villiers proposed as an amendment: "That all duties on imported corn do now cease." It was by no means the wish of the Free-Traders to endanger the Ministerial measure; their object simply was to maintain their consistency by thus entering a protest against the three years' delay. Only 78 members followed Mr. Villiers into the lobby.

The various clauses of the Bill were subjected to a tedious guerilla warfare on the part of the Protectionists, but the second reading was carried on the 27th of March by a majority of 88. In the course of the final debate Sir Robert Peel, at the conclusion of an eloquent speech, said, "I am not surprised to hear honourable members predict that my tenure of power is short. But let us pass this measure, and while it is in progress let me request of you to suspend your indignation. This measure being once passed, you on this side, and you on the opposite side of the House, may adopt whatever measures you think proper for the purpose of terminating my political existence. I assure you I deplore the loss of your confidence much more than I shall deplore the loss of political power. . . . . When I do fall, I shall have the satisfaction of reflecting that I do not fall because I have shown subservience to a party. I shall not fall because I preferred the interests of party to the general interests of the community; and I shall carry with me the satisfaction of reflecting that during the course of my official career my object has been to mitigate monopoly, to increase the demand for industry, to remove the restrictions on commerce, to equalise the burden of taxation, and to ameliorate the condition of those who labour."

At last this important Bill, the largest measure of commercial freedom that had yet been won, the final and fatal blow to a protective policy, and which led to a rapid clearance of what vestiges of it might still remain, reached its closing stage. On the 15th of May, at four o'clock in the morning, the third reading was passed by 327 votes to 229—a majority of 98. Its progress through the House of Lords was rapid and triumphant. Both the Customs' Duties Bill and the Corn Bill were, on the 25th of June, read a third time and passed; and on the 26th they received the Royal assent.

This crowning triumph, after such arduous struggles and under circumstances so peculiar, formed a fitting and honourable close to Sir Robert Peel's Ministerial career. On the 21st of June, in anticipation of the favourable verdict of the House of Lords a few days after, he addressed a memorandum to his colleagues in the Cabinet, in which he submitted for their consideration "whether, after the passing of the Corn and Customs' Bills, it would be for the interest of the Crown, of the country, and for the honour and character of the Government, that they should remain in office." He added, with characteristic sagacity, "A Government ought to have a natural support; a Conservative Government should be supported by a Conservative party. Support from the compassion of its enemies, or even from the personally friendly feelings of those who ought, on public principle, to oppose a Government, is a hollow and not a creditable support. Depend upon it that we shall not pass the Irish Bill into a law. . . . . I am decidedly of opinion that we ought not to retain office after we have lost power." These views met with the concurrence of nearly all the other members of Government. If, having a motive, they wanted a pretext for resigning, they had not long to wait.

The privations and sufferings of a large portion of the Irish population, consequent upon the failure of the potato crop, had resulted in a frightful increase of agrarian violence and crime. The number of these offences in 1844 had been 1,495; in 1845 it was 3,642, and it was now increasing at a rapid rate. To arrest the evil, Government, at an early period of the Session, brought in a bill "for the protection of life and property in Ireland," conferring on the Executive great coercive powers. It was introduced and passed in the House of Lords, whence it was transferred to the arena of the House of Commons. There it was proposed on the 30th of March, by Sir James Graham, and after a strenuous and protracted opposition, the first reading had passed on the 1st of May by a majority of 149.

Sir Robert Peel then named the 25th of May for the second reading, but other pressing matters intervened, and the debate on the second reading only took place on the 9th of June. It commenced languidly, was adjourned from time to time, and on two occasions narrowly escaped a premature end by a count out. At a later period, however, of these adjourned discussions, a rumour became current that the Liberal and Protectionist parties had coalesced for the purpose of rejecting the bill and ousting the Ministry. The excitement thereupon became intense. Lord John Russell declared that the rumour was untrue, and that his opposition was founded on views of his own, not on concert with others. It might be so, but if there was no combination of design, there was unity of action. There may have been no assignation between the parties, but they did, in fact, meet in the same lobby.

Lord G. Bentinck delivered a violent philippic against Sir Robert Peel. He called on the Opposition members, who might indeed have profited by the treason, but could not surely honour the traitor, to join the Protectionists in punishing him. "It is time," he exclaimed, "that atonement should be made to the betrayed honour of Parliament and the betrayed constituencies of the empire." Mr. Cobden closed the debate by a masterly speech. He and his friends would vote against the measure on its own inherent merits, certainly not from any want of confidence in the Minister. "If the division this night be adverse to the Government, then," added he, "I will say that should the right hon. baronet choose to retire from office in consequence of that vote, he carries with him the esteem and gratitude of a larger number of the

1846. population of this empire than ever followed any Minister that was hurled from power. . . . I tender to the right honourable baronet my heartfelt thanks for the unwearied perseverance, the unswerving firmness, and the great ability with which he has, during the last six months, conducted one of the most magnificent reforms ever carried in any country, through this House of Commons."

The division took place on the 26th June, and as had been expected, indeed we might almost say hoped, by both the vanquished and the victors, it sounded the knell of the Peel administration. For the second reading there voted 219 members, against it 294, being a majority of 73 against Ministers. By a coincidence which, whether it was designed or accidental, was interesting and suggestive, the bill for the repeal of the Corn Laws passed the House of Lords on the very same day that the House of Commons overthrew the Ministry by which the bill had been introduced.

CHAPTER XIII.

(*From* 1846 *onwards.*)

Lord John Russell's Administration—Dissolution of the Anti-Corn-Law League—Measures to Relieve Irish Distress—Repeal of the Navigation Laws—Gradual Abolition of remaining Protective Duties—Final Achievement of a thorough Free Trade Tariff.

ON the 29th of June, Sir Robert Peel announced to the House that the Ministers had resigned, in a noble and eloquent speech, some passages of which will never be recalled without exciting interest and sympathy. Such for instance are those which occur towards the conclusion of his address. "In proposing," he said, "those measures of commercial policy which disentitled us to the confidence of many of our former supporters, we were influenced by no other desire than that of promoting the interests of the country. . . . The love of power was not the motive for the proposal of those measures; for I had not a doubt that, whether these measures were attended with failure or with success, one event must certainly occur, and that was the termination of the existence of this Government. . . . I am far from complaining of it; anything is preferable to attempting to maintain ourselves in office without a full measure of the confidence of this House. . . . I have no wish to rob any person of the credit which may be justly due to him in carrying these measures. But I may say, that neither the gentlemen sitting on the benches opposite, nor myself, nor the gentlemen sitting around me—I say that neither of us are the parties who are strictly entitled to the merit. There is a name that ought to be associated with the success of the measures. . . . It is the name of a man who, acting, I believe, from pure and disinterested motives, has advocated their cause with untiring energy, and by appeals to reason, enforced by an eloquence the more to be admired because it was unaffected and unadorned—the name which ought to be, and which will be, associated with the success of these measures is the name of Richard Cobden. (Loud cheers.) . . . I shall surrender power, severely

1846. censured, I fear, by many honourable men who, from no interested motives, have adhered to the principles of protection, because they looked upon them as important to the interests and welfare of the country. I shall leave a name execrated, I know, by every monopolist—(loud cheers and laughter)—who would maintain protection for his own individual benefit. But it may be that I shall leave a name sometimes remembered with expressions of goodwill in the abodes of those whose lot it is to labour and to earn their daily bread by the sweat of their brow, when they shall recruit their exhausted strength with abundant and untaxed food, the sweeter because it is no longer leavened by a sense of injustice." These parting words, at once so earnest and so dignified, were received with hearty and prolonged cheering from all sides of the House.

When after the adjournment of the House to the 3rd of July, Sir Robert Peel left Westminster Hall, leaning on the arm of Sir G. Clerk, he found a large concourse of people waiting outside to see him. "Every head was bared, the crowd made way for him, and many accompanied him in respectful silence to the door of his house."

The task of forming an administration naturally devolved on Lord John Russell, who faithfully carried out the programme of the great Minister whom he succeeded.

Thus expired that enterprising and innovating government, after fulfilling, to a remarkable extent, its principal mission. For, so large was the measure of fiscal reform which it contributed, that the rest had become of easy accomplishment, and indeed, followed in necessary sequence. The edifice of protection was so nearly demolished, that there remained little to be done except to cart away the rubbish. The work commenced by Huskisson twenty years before, had been virtually completed by Peel, and within that short period, the commercial policy of England had been not merely modified, but positively reversed.

Previous, however, to commenting on the effects of that radical revolution, let us proceed briefly to record the removal in rapid succession of every surviving vestige of the old restrictive system. It will be seen that as experience developed the beneficial effects of the earlier reforms, the later ones encountered diminished opposition, and that finally England became one free port, open without restrictions and without duties, to all the commodities of all the nations of the earth.

Immediately after the Ministerial crisis, the leaders of the Anti-Corn-Law League decided on bringing their operations to a close. They held a meeting on the 2nd of July in the Manchester Town Hall. Richard Cobden addressed them, and after congratulating them on the success which they had achieved, he said, speaking of Sir Robert Peel, "If he has lost office, he has gained a country. For my part, I would rather descend into private life with that last measure of his in my hand, than mount to the highest pinnacle of human power." He concluded by moving "That an act of Parliament having been passed, providing for the abolition of the Corn Laws in February, 1849, it is deemed expedient to suspend the

1846. active operations of the Anti-Corn-Law League; and the executive council is hereby requested to take the necessary steps for making up and closing the affairs of the League with as little delay as possible." It was subsequently resolved "that after the payment of the first instalment (20 per cent.), the subscribers to the £250,000 League Fund be released from all further liabilities." After settling some matters of detail, the proceedings of the meeting, and indeed the proceedings of the League itself, closed by Mr. Cobden's reminding them that they were under obligations to the Queen, who was said to have favoured their cause as one of humanity and justice; and their last act before finally separating was to give three hearty cheers for her Majesty.

In this simple and unostentatious manner did this powerful body decree its own dissolution. In the flush of triumph, in the plenitude of their political influence, with a fund of £200,000 at command—with an organisation so complex and yet so complete, that it had made them a power in the state—falsifying by their moderation the predictions of their enemies and justifying their own professions—seeking no thanks, courting no applause—one week after the accomplishment of their mission, these honest-minded men quietly abdicated their self-imposed functions, and voluntarily relinquished the high position which they had gained by eight years' incessant labour and great personal sacrifices. Can history furnish any example of a body of private individuals uniting so effectually, acquiring such influence, achieving such success, and exercising such ready self-denial?

The two ensuing years, 1847 and 1848, were so exclusively devoted to framing the measures necessitated by the famine in Ireland, that the Legislature could spare neither the time nor the labour required in order to perfect the free-trade system. The extent of that dire calamity was beyond all precedent, and it was confronted by efforts equally unparalleled. Upwards of £7,000,000 of money was advanced by Government to meet the exigency. The private subscriptions amounted to £668,000, and to effect the distribution of the funds was the work of many thousands of officials and volunteers. It was soon found that payment of money was liable to gross abuse, and that rations of cooked food formed the safest and most effectual mode of administering relief. We will close our reference to this distressing subject by a quotation from a writer in the *Edinburgh Review* of that period: " This enterprise (organised relief) was in truth the grandest attempt ever made to grapple with famine over a whole country. Organised armies, amounting altogether to some hundreds of thousands, had been rationed before; but neither ancient nor modern history can furnish a parallel to the fact that upwards of three millions of persons were fed every day in the neighbourhood of their own homes by administrative arrangements emanating from and controlled by one central office."

Two days after the opening of Parliament in January, 1847, Lord John Russell adverted to the necessity, under the circumstances, for a rapid supply of cheap food, and moved for leave to bring in bills to

1848, 1849. suspend the operation of the Corn Importation Act and the Navigation Laws till the 1st of September in the same year. This motion was seconded by Mr. Bankes, one of the most ardent of the Protectionists, who pointed out that suspension and abolition were two very distinct things, and that while his party were strenuous opponents of the latter, the former, as a temporary measure to meet a temporary emergency, had their willing concurrence. The motion passed unopposed. The only other step taken this Session in the direction of commercial reform was a proposal made by Mr. Ricardo, on the 9th of February, 1847, for the appointment of a select committee to inquire into the operation of the Navigation Laws. This was resisted by the Protectionists, but, being supported by both Lord J. Russell and Sir Robert Peel, it was carried by a large majority. As is usual, inquiry revealed the errors and defects of the restrictive system, and, as is not quite so usual, led, in this case, to a thorough reform. This reform was embodied in a Bill introduced by Mr. Labouchere during the session of 1848. But although the principle was affirmed, yet the attention of the House was so absorbed by Irish affairs, that the Bill remained in abeyance till the following year.

The Queen's Speech, on the opening of Parliament on the 2nd of February, 1849, contained the following paragraph : " I again commend to your attention the restrictions imposed on commerce by the Navigation Laws. If you shall find that these laws are in whole or in part unnecessary for the maintenance of our maritime power, while they fetter trade and industry, you will no doubt deem it right to repeal or modify their provisions." This suggestion, and the bill introduced in conformity with it, met with the strenuous opposition of the Protectionist party. All their other positions had been forced one by one, and they now took their stand upon this as their last entrenchment. Their prophecies of ruin to the British Navy, national as well as mercantile, their indignant wrath at the Free-traders thus fostering foreign at the expense of British industry, their wailings over the departing glories of the British Empire were depressingly mournful. How agreeably disappointed they must have been in after years when they found themselves so egregiously wrong!

Mr. H. Drummond said that the "end and intentions of the Manchester school were to discharge all British labourers, and to employ foreign labourers in lieu of them."

Mr. Herries deprecated these attacks on "a system which was the nursery of our flourishing mercantile marine, the foundation of our naval supremacy, and which, if once abandoned for the sake of a rash experiment, could never be restored."

Mr. T. Baring called on all those "who attached any importance to the national safety, to vote against a bill which he believed was forced upon a reluctant people and a hesitating Parliament."

But in spite of all opposition and of all sensational appeals, the bill passed in both Houses of Parliament. The commerce of the United Kingdom —indeed, five years later the coasting trade itself— recognised no difference whatever between British and foreign vessels. Our ports were open to all on equal terms. A French or American line of steamers is quite free to trade between (for instance) Newcastle and London. No distinction of nationality is made. The cheapest, quickest, safest, ships obtain the preference, and thus the nation enjoys the benefits that accrue from the cheapness, rapidity, and safety with which we and our goods are conveyed to our destinations. It was thus that England of her own accord, urged by no external pressure, making no bargains for reciprocity, in simple conformity with the dictates of economic science, abolished her monopoly, and trusted to her own energies to withstand the free competition of the world.

The contest on the Navigation Laws was the last pitched battle fought by the Protectionist party. Their resistance grew fainter and fainter, and a few occasional skirmishes just reminded the world that such a party still existed.

Three years afterwards their leaders came into power. In February, 1852, the Earl of Derby became Prime Minister, and Mr. Disraeli Chancellor of the Exchequer and leader of the House of Commons. The Free-traders, alarmed at the possibility of some attempt to reverse the policy of commercial freedom which had been adopted, took the earliest opportunity of questioning those Ministers in Parliament on the subject. The discreet reply was that the Government did not intend to propose any return to the policy of protection during the present Session, nor at any future time, unless a great majority of members favourable to that policy should be returned to Parliament.

But far from this proving to be the case, the general election which immediately ensued reinstated a Liberal Government, and the work of stripping off the few rags of protection that still hung on went rapidly forward.

On the 18th of April, 1853, Mr. Gladstone, as Chancellor of the Exchequer, made his financial statement in an able and luminous speech. Such was the admirable order in which he marshalled his topics, and the transparent lucidity with which he treated them, that although his address occupied five hours in the delivery, and although it bristled with figures and statistics, he never for a moment lost the attention or fatigued the minds of his hearers. Mr. Gladstone's financial scheme included, among other reforms, the reduction or total remission of imposts on 133 articles. In this way, our tariff underwent rapid simplification.

Each subsequent year was marked by a similar elimination of protective impediments to free commercial intercourse with other countries. In 1860, butter, cheese, &c., were admitted duty free; in 1869, the small nominal duty that had been left on corn was abolishéd; in 1874, sugar was relieved from the remnant of duty that had survived from previous reductions.

It would be superfluous, as well as tedious, to enter upon a detailed reference to the various minor reforms through which we advanced towards, and finally reached, our present free-trade tariff. In fact, all the great battles had been fought and won by the close of the year 1849, and the struggle was then virtually over.

We have endeavoured in these pages faithfully to record the inception, progress, and triumph of the free-trade movement. But there still remains for us the task of defining and describing the position to which we have been led by that movement. Is our present tariff one from which every shred and vestige of protection have been discarded? Is it truly and thoroughly a free-trade tariff? That these questions must be answered in the affirmative it is easy to prove in the most conclusive manner. We raise about £20,000,000 of our annual revenue by means of customs' duties on the foreign commodities which we import, and this fact is sometimes adduced by the advocates for protection, without any explanation, leaving their readers to infer that ours is not, as it really is, a free-trade tariff. That such an inference is totally erroneous will presently be made manifest beyond all question.

We now levy import duties on only fifteen articles. Subjoined is a list of them, and to each is appended the amount of duty levied on it during the financial year ending 1st of April, 1879.

Articles Imported, not Produced in England.

Tobacco	£8,589,681
Tea	4,169,233
Wine	1,469,710
Dried Fruit	509,234
Coffee	212,002
Chicory	66,739
Chocolate and Cocoa	44,671
	£15,061,270

ARTICLES IMPORTED, PRODUCED ALSO IN ENGLAND.

Spirits	£5,336,058
Plate (Silver and Gold)	5,853
Beer	3,814
Vinegar	671
Playing Cards	522
Pickles	17
Malt	6
Spruce	3
	£5,346,944

£20,408,214

It will be seen by the above figures that £15,000,000, or three-fourths of the total sum levied, is levied on articles which we do not and cannot produce in England. It is clear, therefore, that this portion of the import duties cannot by any possibility be said to afford the slightest "protection to native industry." Every shilling's worth which we consume of those articles comes from abroad, and every shilling extra that the consumer pays for them in consequence of the duty goes to the revenue. So much for that portion of the £20,400,000 import duties.

As to the £5,336,000 levied on foreign spirits, it consists of import duties which are only the exact counterpart of the excise duties levied internally on the produce of the British distillers. The foreign article is placed on precisely the same footing as the native article. Both have to pay the same duty of about 10s. per gallon on spirits of the same strength. It would of course be an absurb stultification to admit foreign spirits duty-free while the English producer was burdened with a tax of 10s. per gallon; but by making the excise duty and the customs' duty precisely the same, equality is established, and no protection or preference whatever is enjoyed by the native distiller. The excise duty levied in the aforesaid year ending April, 1879, on spirits the produce of British distilleries, was no less than £14,855,000. The trifling amounts raised on plate, beer, vinegar, &c., are explained in the same way. They also act as a mere counterpoise to the excise duties levied on the British producers of the same articles, and thus afford to the latter no protection whatever against foreign competition.

It is evident, therefore, that our tariff does not retain within it one solitary shred of protection. Foreigners may send us what article they like, in what quantities they like, and it is admitted free of any protective duty whatever. If the foreigner can produce an article cheaper than we can produce it ourselves, we freely and readily buy it of him, knowing full well that, as all commerce is barter, and our purchases will be paid for in goods and not in gold, if we buy his cheap article, we must and shall export in return an extra quantity of some other of our own goods. In that way we secure the unalloyed benefit of buying in the cheapest market wherever that may be, whether at home or abroad.

It may be observed that out of the revenue from import duties of £20,400,000, about £19,000,000 was derived from four articles only; and of these, three of them—tobacco, wine, and spirits—which are articles of sheer luxury, and therefore fair objects of taxation—

contributed £15,400,000. It were greatly to be desired that the £4,400,000 raised on tea and coffee could be dispensed with, but this is a mere domestic question of revenue, which we cannot discuss here. What we wished to show, and what we think we have shown beyond all doubt or cavil, is that our present short list of articles subject to import duties forms a thoroughly free-trade tariff, in the truest and fullest sense.

CHAPTER XIV.

Effects of Free Trade on the Prosperity of the Country—Comparative Condition of England in 1840 under Protection, and in 1878 under Free Trade—Concluding Remarks.

WE need hardly point out the striking contrast which our present commercial policy exhibits to that which prevailed at the period when this short history commences. In about a quarter of a century we have moved on from a thoroughly restrictive to a thoroughly free-trade system. This movement has been slow, but continuous. Our early steps were hesitating and tentative, but, encouraged by experience, and finding that practice justified theory, our progress became more rapid, and marching forward in an accelerated ratio, we at last effected a final and decisive change. For good or for evil our fiscal policy underwent a complete revolution. What was the result of this revolution on our national welfare? Have we to lament, or to congratulate ourselves upon, our abandonment of the old system of monopoly and exclusiveness? Let us devote a few pages to this inquiry.

The way to proceed will be briefly to compare the state of the country in the year 1840 with its state in 1878. We select 1840, because it was one of the most prosperous years under the old protective policy. On the other hand, 1878 was a year of commercial depression, so that the comparison rests on the most favourable data for the old policy. If the change from that to a free-trade policy had been inimical to the interests of the nation, the evil would manifest itself in the shape of diminished trade, diminished wealth, diminished prosperity, and arrested progress. But if, instead of such a result, the trade, wealth, prosperity, and progress of the United Kingdom should, under the new system of commercial freedom, have enormously increased—increased in a ratio far beyond that of any former period, and of any other country—it must then be conceded that the previsions of the enlightened statesmen who effected the change have been justified by the event.

Let us collect a few data for forming our judgment.

POPULATION.—In 1840, the population of the United Kingdom was 26,487,000; in 1878, it was estimated at 33,799,000. Increase, 7,312,000. In the former year London contained 1,700,000 inhabitants; in the latter 3,800,000. Increase, 2,100,000. So that the growth of London during the last 38 years alone, largely exceeded the total growth it had attained during the previous thousand years. In 1878, the emigration of British subjects to America, Australia, and all other places, comprised 112,902 persons. The number who embarked at our ports for those places was much greater, but it consisted largely of emigrants from Germany and other Continental States, who took their way through this country for the convenience of passage. On the other hand, the number of immigrants in 1878 was 77,951, many of them being returned emigrants; so that, on the balance, the yearly exodus from the United Kingdom is much smaller than is generally imagined.

TRADE.—In 1840, the foreign trade of the United Kingdom (combined exports and imports) amounted to £172,133,000, equivalent to £6 9s. 11½d. per head of the population. In 1878, it amounted to £614,255,000, or £18 3s. 6d. per head, a marvellous rate of increase! In the United States the proportion of foreign trade to the population is £4 13s. per head. In France, it was in 1876 £8 3s. per head. In Russia it was, in 1876, £1 9s. per head.

REVENUE.—The public revenue for the year 1840 was £51,850,000; for the year 1878, £81,598,000; and the latter sum presses far less heavily on the people now than did the former sum on the people then. The income-tax in 1843 (the first year of its incidence) yielded, for every penny in the pound, £801,000. In 1878 the taxable incomes had so increased, that every penny in the pound of income-tax yielded £1,947,000.

CONSUMPTION PER HEAD.—Of those articles which are partly produced at home and partly imported, the consumption per head cannot be exactly ascertained, because the extent of the home production cannot be accurately defined. But of those articles consumed by the people, which are wholly imported from abroad, the consumption per head is easily calculated, and it is as follows for the two years which we have taken for comparison:—

CONSUMPTION PER HEAD OF THE POPULATION OF THE UNITED KINGDOM IN 1840 AND 1878 OF THE FOLLOWING ARTICLES:—

	1840.	1878.
Tea	1·22 lbs.	4·66 lbs
Sugar (raw)	15·20 ,,	48·56 ,,
Coffee	1·08 ,,	0·97 ,,
Rice	0·90 ,,	7·50 ,,
Currants and Raisins	1·45 ,,	4·49 ,,
Tobacco	0·86 ,,	1·45 ,,

The immensely improved condition of the working classes of this country is clearly shown by the above table; for the wealthy and middle classes must have consumed nearly as much per head of tea, sugar, &c., in 1840 as they do now, and therefore it is chiefly among the wage-receivers of the community that the largely increased consumption has been distributed.

SAVINGS BANKS.—The deposits in these banks, which are national institutions, consist of individually small sums, being savings invested voluntarily by the wage-earners of the community. In 1841 the amount of these deposits (after deducting withdrawals) was £24,475,000; in 1878 it was £75,967,000. This large increment has been gradual and continuous, and affords another distinct proof of the enhanced prosperity of the working classes since the advent of free trade.

PAUPERISM.—The number of adult able-bodied paupers who were receiving relief in England and Wales on the 1st of January, 1849, was 201,644, out of a population of 17,565,000. On the 1st of January,

1878, the number had diminished to 97,927, out of a population of 24,854,000. We have been obliged to take the year 1849 for comparison, because it is the first year for which the actual number of persons receiving relief on a given day was returned; and the comparison is confined to England and Wales because no returns exist for Scotland and Ireland. The number of paupers from age, infirmity, sickness, &c., had also largely decreased in proportion to the population.

CRIME.—In 1840 the convictions for criminal offences of all kinds throughout the United Kingdom were 34,030, with a population of 26,487,000. In 1878 they were 17,038, with a population of 33,799,000. That is to say, that during those thirty-eight years crime had diminished in this country by one-half, while the population had increased by 7,300,000. Could there be a stronger proof of the vast moral as well as material progress of the people? Note, also, that this decrease of crime was no sudden, fitful, or accidental circumstance, but was the gradual result, year after year, of permanent influences.

WEALTH.—An eminent statist, Mr. R. Giffen, has, by a series of elaborate calculations, arrived at the conclusion that in 1875 the total capital of the people of the United Kingdom might be reckoned as a minimum at £8,500,000,000. "This," he says, "is the capitalised value of the income derived from capital, using as far as possible the data of the income-tax returns as the basis of the estimate, and with the addition of an estimate of the amount of capital in use not yielding an income." By a similar process he has made out that the total capital of the country in 1865 was £6,100,000,000, and, consequently, that during the intervening ten years the national estate had improved at the rate of £240,000,000 per annum. In 1875 the amount assessed to the income-tax was £571,000,000; in 1865 it was £396,000,000. Now in 1843, when the income-tax was imposed, the amount assessed to it was only £251,000,000. Let us, then, take the proportion between the taxable income and the national capital as given by Mr. Giffen for the two periods 1865 and 1875, and apply it to the £251,000,000 taxable income of 1843, and we shall find that it gives £3,880,000,000 as the total capital of the country in 1843. This, of course, is only an approximate valuation, but it cannot be far wrong, and it leads to the conclusion that the capital of the country has far more than doubled since 1840, while the increase of the population has only been 28 per cent. This enormous mass of wealth makes our national debt an easy burden compared with its pressure in 1840, and the process of accumulation is still going on at the average rate of at least £200,000,000 per annum.

COMMERCIAL MARINE.—The fluctuations in our progress under this head are curious and characteristic. In 1840, the tonnage of the registered vessels of the United Kingdom was 2,571,000 tons. In 1849, when our protective Navigation Laws were repealed, the tonnage was 3,096,000, an increase, under the old system, of 525,000 tons in nine years. In 1849 our trade was thrown open to the shipping of all the world, and our ship-owners and ship-builders were told that they would be swept away by the competition. What happened? In 1858, nine years after the repeal of the Navigation Laws, the tonnage of the registered vessels of the United Kingdom was 4,325,000, an increase of 1,229,000 tons over the tonnage of 1849. So that while during the nine years of protection that preceded 1849 the increase was 525,000 tons, the increase during the nine years of unrestricted competition that followed 1849 was 1,229,000 tons; and the expansion of our mercantile navy has been going on ever since. In 1878 the tonnage of the United Kingdom was 6,236,000, and the greatest part of the entire international trade of the world is conducted in British bottoms. To afford some insight into the present distribution of the carrying trade, we may state that the total tonnage of the vessels that discharged and reloaded cargoes in 1878 at the various ports of the United Kingdom was 42,900,000 tons, of which 30,297,000 were British and 12,603,000 were foreign. These 12,603,000 tons of foreign shipping were distributed as follows:—

Norwegian	2,444,000 Tons.
German	2,270,000 ,,
Swedish	1,133,000 ,,
Danish	1,058,000 ,,
United States of America	988,000 ,,
Italian	981,000 ,,
All other countries	3,729,000 ,,
	12,603,000 ,,

Thus we have taken stock, as it were, of the material condition of the people of England at the two periods referred to, viz., 1840 under protection, and 1878 under free trade. The progress that the nation has made in wealth and prosperity during those thirty-eight years seems almost incredible, and one is tempted to think that the picture that has been traced of that progress is the work of a heated imagination. But, no! The statements made rest on the solid foundation of attested facts and the unimpeachable testimony of official records. Their truth may be tested by every one who chooses to inquire.

And yet, inconceivable as it may appear, there are men among the foreign advocates of protection who gravely assert that England has, since her adoption of free trade, been in a state of gradual decay, and is now on the eve of utter prostration! A cause which needs such advocacy as this must indeed be feeble.

It is in no boastful spirit that we have put forth these statements as to the progress of our country. We were, by the very nature of our work, compelled to inquire into the effect of the free-trade system on our national condition, and we have only portrayed the sober truth as disclosed by statistical evidence. That the result of the investigation should exhibit, in so striking a manner, the success that has attended the adoption of commercial freedom in England is, it must be allowed, an interesting and suggestive fact. We have accordingly written in a spirit of thankfulness for having advanced thus far, and of hopefulness that we shall advance farther. We know but too well how immeasurably distant we and all other nations are from political and social perfection. As long as ignorance, poverty, preventible disease, and crime defile the face of the land, so long is the work of the statesman incomplete.

And that work, judging from the past, will take the direction, less of good laws to be passed, than of bad laws to be abrogated. Governments have hitherto been chiefly occupied in doing mischief and in partially undoing it. Nearly all the beneficial, comprehensive, and popular measures enacted by our parliaments have been repeals of previous enactments. Our legislative dealings in regard to Catholic emancipation, the Reform Bill, the Test and Corporation Acts, the Corn Laws, the restrictive import duties, the Navigation Laws, &c.—measures of primary importance which have remoulded the destinies of the country—were all of them repeals of pre-existing laws.

There are three prevailing errors which we think that the perusal of these pages will effectually dispel. 1. The notion that we adopted free trade under the pressure of necessity, and not from deliberate conviction. 2. The notion that ours is not a thorough free-trade tariff. 3. The notion that the prosperity of England has suffered a decline under the influence of the free-trade system. In regard to the latter, even those who, not denying our prosperity, deny its connection with free-trade, must admit that if our change of policy did not cause, it certainly did not prevent, our rapid advance in the path of improvement. They may question whether our onward progress has been the result, but they must at least allow that it has been the concomitant, of free-trade.

Our task is done. We have described the position from which the free-trade movement started, as also the position to which it has borne us, and we have narrated the chief incidents by which the transition from the one to the other has been marked. We have at the same time endeavoured to do justice to the men through whose instrumentality the triumph of free-trade has been achieved, and to whom a debt of gratitude is owing, not only by Englishmen, but by the world at large. For that the world at large will, sooner or later, participate in the material prosperity which unrestricted commercial freedom confers, is as certain as it is that the deductions of science cannot long be ignored, and that, in the end, truth must universally prevail.

THE END.

INDEX.

ABOLITION of Corn Duties proposed by Villiers, 62
—— of Slavery, 14
Address to Queen moved by Duncombe, 73
Adjourned Debate of Feb. 14, 1842, 61
Advance of Peel Ministry in Free Trade Principles, 96
Agriculturists declare against Peel, 70
Amendment to Peel's Resolutions, 1846, 153
Amendments respecting Income Tax, 67
Announcement of Intended Repeal of Corn Laws in *Times*, Dec. 4, 1845, 141
Anti-Corn-Law Association, Formation of, 20
—— Circular, 26, 36
—— League, Formation of, 25
—— Meetings disturbed by Chartists, 57
Apology for Peel's conduct in 1845-6, 147
Apparent Combination of Protectionists and Liberals against Peel, 161
Appeal of Chartist Leaders, 74
Articles imported but also produced in England, 173
—— now subject to Import Duty, 173
—— of luxury fairly taxed, 174
Assassination of Mr. Drummond, 81
Assertions of Foreign Advocates of Protection untenable, 182
BAD HARVEST of 1845, 133
"Balance of Trade"—its meaning, 8
Bank Charter renewed by Peel, 111
Banquet in St. Peter's Fields, Manchester, 30
Bazaar in aid of Funds of League, 1842, 56
Bentinck's Philippics against Peel, 151, 161
Bill "for Protection of Life and Property in Ireland," 1846, 160
Blackstone and the Agriculturists, 91
Bramston and Duty on Grease, 124
Bowring's, Dr., Speech on the Corn Laws, 19
BRIGHT, JOHN :—
  Appeal to Operatives on Strike, 77
  Defence of Peel, Feb., 1846, 156
  Distinctive Characteristics of, 96
  Returned for Durham (City), 93
  Speech at Covent Garden Theatre, 84, 114
CABINET COUNCIL of Oct. 31, 1845, 137
Canadian Wheat, Proposal respecting, 93
Catholic Emancipation, 14
Causes of general distress, 1841, 53
—— of success of League, 56
Change of Public Opinion on Fiscal Reform, 39
Chartist Agitation, 1842, 74

Chartists opposed to Anti-Corn-Law League, 37
——, Leaders of the, 37
Clay's Motion for Modification of Corn Laws, 17
Cobbett and the "Pauperising Root," 135
COBDEN, RICHARD :—
  Address voted to, 85
  Attack on Landowners by, 92
  Cosmopolitan Principles of, 51
  Distinguishing Characteristics of, 49
  Efforts as Free-Trader, 26
  First Appearance as Free-Trader, 21
  First in Parliament, 49
  Imputation on, of inciting to Assassination, 83
  Influence of, purely personal, 51
  In Personal Intercourse, 50
  Mission to the Farmers, 1843, 94
  Motion for Inquiry into cause of Agricultural Distress, 1845, 119
  Motion for Inquiry into Effect of Protective Duties, 107
  Sarcasm on Agricultural Members, 124
  Secret of his Oratorical Power, 49
  Speech at Warrington, 37
  —— of Oct. 6, 1842, 78
  —— on Peel's Sliding Scale, 63
  —— at Manchester, 84
  Spirited Appeal to Peel, 73
  —— to Delegates, 34
  Stirring Appeal to Country Gentlemen, 119
  Strictures on Peel's conduct, 82
Coercion Bill for Ireland, 1846, 160
Comments of Protectionists on League, 86
Commercial Crisis of 1835 and 1836, 12
—— Depression, 1837, 16
—— Marine in 1840 and 1878, 180
—— System in 1834, 1
Comparison of State of Country in 1840 and 1878, 176
Completion of Fund of £100,000, 132
Condition of Agriculturists, 1844, 113
—— Country, 1842, 57
—— Farmers in 1843, 79
—— Manufacturing Districts, 1841, 53
—— People under Restrictive Policy, 9
Conduct of Landed Interest, 1845, 120
Conference at Manchester, 1841, 55
Consequences of "Protection to Native Industries," 54
Conservative Government an "Organised Hypocrisy," 122
Conservatives and Free-Traders, 1839, 19
Consumption per Head in 1840 and 1878, 177
Contending Parties on Fiscal Policy, 1845, 116
Contrast of Condition of Country under Protection and Free Trade, 175

INDEX.

Corn Law of 1815, 5
—— 1822, 5
Cost to Peel of Adoption of Free Trade Principles, 148
Covent Garden Theatre, Meetings at, 98, 114, 132
Crime in 1840 and 1878, 179
"Crown and Anchor" Meeting of League, 58
Customs Duties and Corn Bill passed, 159
Custom Houses, Necessity for, 4
DEBATE on Amendment on Peel's Resolutions, 1846, 153
—— Sugar Duties, 45
—— Villiers' Motion, March, 1839, 25
Decision of House on Sugar Question reversed, 160
Defeat of Miles's Amendment, Feb., 1846, 157
—— Ministry on Sugar Duties, 46
—— Peel Administration on Irish Coercion Bill, 162
—— Sugar Question, 109
—— Russell Administration on Address, 48
Delegates, Deputation of, to Peel, 72
—— Meeting of at Manchester, 55
—— —— in London, 31
—— proceed to House of Commons 59
—— Depression of Agricultural Interest, 1822, 6
Deputations to Lord Melbourne and others, 31
Difficulties of Collecting Revenues, 66
Diminution of Revenue, 1843, 80
Direct Taxation adopted by Peel, 64
Disease in Potatoes first appears, 135
DISRAELI, BENJAMIN :—
  Attacks Peel, 151
  Onslaught on Peel, 121
  Reflections on Peel, 109
  Strictures on Peel justifiable, 123
  Taunts galling to Peel, 123
Dissemination of Publications of League, 55
Dissolution of Anti-corn-law League, 166
Distress prevalent throughout Country, 1842, 70
Drouyn de Lhuys on Cobden, 51
Drury Lane, Continued Meetings at, 1843, 86, 87
Duke of Buckingham leaves Ministry, 58
Duties on Foreign Spirits, Remarks on, 173
EARL FITZWILLIAM joins League, 100
Effect of Reduction of Silk Duties, 2
English Tariff, Condition of, 1842, 65
Enthusiasm of Members of League, 149
Excitement throughout the Country, 1845, 137
Executive Committee of Anti-Corn-Law League, 22
Expectations from "Balance of Trade," 8
Expense of Collecting Revenue, 4
Extension of Anti-Corn-Law Associations, 22
Extinction of Protection, 165
FAILURE of Chartist Agitation, 71
—— Potato Crop in Ireland, 134
—— the Three W's, 17

Farm Labourers, Wretched Condition of, 112
Farmers' Meetings in 1843, 95
Feargus O'Connor, 76
Fears of Protectionists, 90
Features in Programme of League, 1843-44, 97
Financial Budget for 1841, 43
First Breach in Fortress of Protection, 67
Fiscal Reformers, Action of, 1838, 19
—— Regulations of 1824, 3
Fixed Duty on Corn, why unfair, 42
Fluctuations in Price of Corn, 1836-1843, 80
Foreign Silk Manufacturers prohibited, 10
—— Trade in 1824, 7
Fox (W. J.) at Covent Garden, 98
Free Trade made a Policy, 2
—— Policy not result of Irish Famine, 39
—— Principles of, accepted by Peel, 69
—— Principles, why ultimately adopted, 133
Free Traders not satisfied with Budget, 1845, 118
—— under Cobden and Bright, 116
Fund of £50,000 raised by League, 78
GENERAL ELECTION of 1837, 18
—— of 1841, 47
—— Remarks on Progress from 1840 to 1878, 181
—— Strike proposed by Chartists, 74
GLADSTONE, WILLIAM EWART :—
  Caution respecting Free Trade, 81
  Joins Peel, 144
  Opposes Cobden's Motion, 1844, 107
  Opposition to Villiers' Motion, 88
  Statement, Remarks on, 89
Goulburn's Budget, 1844, 107
—— Motion on Sugar Duties, 1844, 108
Gravitation of Peel and Party to Free Traders, 117
Grogan and Duty on Land
Grounds on which Peel was assailed by his Opponents, 1845-6, 144
HARVEST of 1835 ; Its Effect, 15
—— of 1844, 104
Huskisson, President of Board of Trade, 10
Hume's Committee. Why appointed, 33
IGNORANCE, Poverty, Disease, and Crime yet to be dealt with, 182
Improvement in Trade, 1844, 112
Inauguration of new Policy, 2
Income Tax imposed by Peel, 1842, 64
—— Opposed by Whigs, 67
Import Duties, Effect of, 1
Indecision of Cabinet, 139
Independence of Action claimed by Peel, 52
Indirect Taxation reduced by Peel, 64
"Instructing the Nation," 25
Ireland, State of, 1844—1846, 160
Irish Famine and Free Trade, 40
—— of 1815, 134
JOSEPH HUME'S Committee of Inquiry, 33
KNATCHBULL on Free Trade, 91
LEAGUE, ANTI-CORN-LAW :—
  Action of, in 1844, 113
  Activity of, in 1842, 78

INDEX. 187

LEAGUE, ANTI-CORN-LAW (continued):
And Cobden, 1841, 47
Increased activity of, 55
Influence of, on Registration lists, 113
Literature of, 26
Meeting in London, 1842, 72
Meetings of, in 1841, 38
—— in January, 1845, 115
Opoaition of, to Peel's scheme, 61
Preparations of, for campaign, 1843-4, 97
Styled "a new Power in the State," 103
League newspaper, progress of, 106
Liberals under Palmerston and Russell, 116
Lord Dalhousie joins Peel, 144
—— Derby and Disraeli deny any intention to return to a Protective Policy, 170
—— Howick's Motion, 81
—— Liverpool's Corn Law Act, 6
—— Morpeth at Wakefield, 105
—— Stanley's Measure, 93
Loyd (Lord Overstone) joins League, 99
MACAULAY'S speech on Peel's Measure, 62
Macclesfield, Meeting at, 38
Manchester Association, Action of, 1839, 24
Marquis of Westminster joins League, 105
Marriage of the Queen, 35
Masters, Action of, during Strike of 1842, 76
Meeting at Free Trade Hall, Manchester, 84
—— of League at Manchester, 138, 149
Meetings throughout the Country calling on Government to open Ports, 139
Melbourne Administration, 18
—— Decline, of, 26
Men unlikely to retain same Opinions throughout Life, 145
Miles's Motion, 120
Ministerialists under Peel and Gladstone, 116
Mission of Dr. Lyon Playfair and Professor Lindley to Ireland, 138
Modified Sliding Scale proposed by Peel, 60
Moral Influence of Bazaar held by League at Covent Garden, 127
Morning Herald on League, 103
—— *Post* on Cobden and Protectionists, 93
—— *Pos* on Sir Robert Peel, 103
Municipal Corporations, Reform of, 15
NATIONAL BAZAAR at Covent Garden Theatre, 125
Navigation Laws, Effect of, 1
—— First Breach in, 10
—— Prior to 1815, 7
—— Proposal for Select Committee on, 168
—— Repealed, 1849, 170
Newdegate's Remarks on Cobden, 121
OBJECTIONS to Fiscal Change, 1841, 44
Objects of this volume, 3
Opening of Parliament by Queen 1844, 105
—— Year 1843, 79
Opposition to Penny Postage Scheme, 27
—— Tariff Reform, 70

PAPER DUTY, Abatement in, 16
Parliament Prorogued by Queen, 1843, 97
Parliamentary Debate a Battle, 3
—— Reform, 14
Pattison (Free Trader) returned for London, 100
Paulton's Lectures on Free Trade, 20
Pauperism in 1840 and 1878, 178
PEEL, SIR ROBERT :—
And the Delegates of the League, 59
Angry Reply to Cobden, 82
Announces Change of Opinion on Protection, 150
Arguments for Reduction of Duties, 69
Attack on Duncombe's Motion, 73
Attack on Ministers, 1841, 46
Contemplates extreme Measures, 136
Conversion to Free-trade Principles —inspired by Dictates of Conscience, 145
Defence of Free-trade Principles, 155
Desired by Queen to retain Office, 143
Financial Plans for 1845, 117
In Power, 1841, 52
Letter to Her Majesty, 142
Letter to Wellington, and Reply, 140
Memorandum to Colleagues, June, 1846, 159
Notice with reference to Corn Laws, 1842, 58
On change in Sugar Duties, 45
Policy of Inaction, 80
Political Morality, 123
Power over Protectionists, 110
Proposals to Cabinet Council of Nov. 6, 137
Proposes Total Repeal of Corn Laws for 1849, 152
Reduction of Import Duties, 68
Retention of Leadership of Party Defended, 146
Return to Power in 1845 ineffective to stop Action of League, 148
Shows desire to Abrogate Corn Laws, 140
Sliding Scale, 1842, becomes Law, 64
Speech at Close of Debate, 1846, 158
On Resigning Office, 1846, 163
States Plan of Financial Policy, 151
Still Opposed to Free Trade, 106
Tenders his Resignation, 142
Peel's Bill Passed, May 15, 1846, 159
Penny Postage Adopted Abroad, 28
"People's Charter," 71
Petition for Repeal of Corn Laws, 21
—— in Favour of the Charter, 71
Poor Law Amendment Bill, 14
Population in 1840 and 1878, 176
Potato Crop an Evil to Ireland, 134
Preparations for Campaign of 1845, 116
Present Tariff a Free-trade Tariff, 172
Prevailing Errors that this Volume will tend to Dispel, 183
Progress of Free-trade System Abroad, 28

Proposal for Fixed Duty on Corn, 42
Prorogation of Parliament, 54, 74
Protection Damaged by Ridicule, 125
Protectionists and League, 1842, 78
—— under Stanley and Disraeli, 116
Public Interest in Repeal of Corn Laws Roused, 29

INDEX

Public Meetings on Corn Laws, 25
QUEEN VICTORIA, Accession of, 18
Queen's Speech, 48, 57, 117, 168
Question of Income Tax Carried, 67
REACTION after High Prices, 6
Reasoning of Protectionists, 44
Reasons why Peel asked House to Consent to Repeal of Corn Laws, 153
Reception of Peel's Sliding Scale in large towns, 61
Reduction of Duties on Silk, 11
Relief of Famine in Ireland, 1847—8, 167
Reluctance of Peel's Colleagues to support him, 141
Remission of Duties, 1844, 107
—— by Mr. Gladstone, 1853, 171
Removal of Import Duties sought by League, 66
—— Remaining Vestiges of Restrictive System, 165
Repeal of all Bad Laws desirable and necessary, 183
—— Navigation Laws brought before Parliament, 169
—— Restrictions on Importation of Machinery, 96
Reply to Charge against Peel of changing Opinion on Debatable Point, 144
Report of Work done by League, 1842—3, 97
Repudiation of Protection by Manufacturers, 33
Resignation of Peel Ministry, 1846, 162
Results of Hume's Committee of Inquiry, 34
Revenue in 1840 and 1878, 177
Revision of Tariff, 1842, 64
Revival of Trade, etc., 1844, 104
Rick-burning and Incendiarism, 1844, 112
Roebuck's Objection to Stanley's Proposal, 94
Rowland Hill's Penny Postage Scheme, 27
RUSSELL, LORD JOHN:—
Amendment on Peel's Proposal for the Sliding Scale, 62
Attack on Protective Duties, 127
Attempt to form a Government, Dec. 18th, 1845, 142
Causes of his Failure, 143
Letter to Electors of City of London, 139
Motion of May 30th, 1841, 41
Reply to Knatchbull, 91
Restriction and Monopoly opposed by, 128
Resolutions on Condition of the Working Classes, 127
Opposed by Peel and Graham, 129
Speech in favour of Free Trade, 1846, 158
Succeeds Peel in Office, July, 1846, 164
SAVINGS BANKS in 1840 and 1878, 178
Scene between Peel and Cobden, 81
Session of 1846 opened by Queen, 150
Semi-Official adoption of Free Trade Principles, 37
Shift in Sliding Scale, 1828, 13
Sincerity of Peel's Convictions, 145
Six Points of Charter, 36

Sophistry of Arguments for Protection, 45
Specific Proposal for New Law by Peel, 141
Speech of Cobden in Manchester, July, 1846, 165
Speeches of Baring, Miles, and Peel, in Great Debate of Feb., 1846, 154
—— Cobden and Bentinck, Feb., 1846, 157
—— Cobden, Bright, and Fox, at Covent Garden, June 18, 1845, 132
—— for and against Villiers' Resolutions, 1845, 131
Spitalfields Weavers, Riot by, 11
Stamp Duty, Reduction of, 16
Stanley, Withdrawal of, from Peel's Ministry, 144
State of the Country, 1841, 53
Strike in Scotland, Wales, Yorkshire, &c., 1842, 77
—— of Operatives in Lancashire, 76
Struggle with Peel abandoned by Landlords, 146
Subscriptions to £100,000 Fund of League, 101
Substance of Villiers' Resolutions, 1845, 130
Success of Free Trade promoted by the Famine in Ireland, 126
Sugar Duties, Proposed Reduction of, 43
Sum of £150,000 raised by Anti-Corn-Law League, 149
—— raised by Bazaar at Covent Garden, 126
Summary of Budget, 1845, 118
Suspension of Corn Importation Act, 1847, 167
TACTICS of Free-Traders, 1840, 29
Tariff List of United Kingdom, 4
——, Revision of, 65
Taxation of Foreign Labour, 8
Timber Duties, Proposed Change in, 43
Times on Subscriptions to League, 101
Tithe Commutation Act, 1836, 16
Trade in 1840 and 1878, 177
VILLIERS, C. P.:—
Amendment, 1842, Rejection of, 64
—— to Ministerial Measure, March, 1846, 158
Annual Motion on Corn Laws, 23, 32, 88, 111, 129
Public Dinner to, 21
Vote of Want of Confidence, 46
Voting Registers, Revision of by League, 113
WAKEFIELD, Meeting at, 1844, 105
Warrington, Meeting at, 39
Ward and Ricardo, Motions by, 1843, 87
Wealth in 1840 and 1878, 179
Wellington, Duke of, in Power, 131
What has been done in this Book, 183
Whig Budget of 1841, 35
Whigs and Tories united against Fiscal Reform, 29
Wheat, Current Prices of, 1836—1845, 50
——, Price of, in 1816 and 1817, 5
——, Rise in Price of, Aug. 1845, 134
William IV., Death of, 17
Wood and Manchester Chamber of Commerce, 23
Work done by Anti-Corn-Law League, 85

www.ingramcontent.com/pod-product-compliance
Lightning Source LLC
Chambersburg PA
CBHW020053200426
43197CB00050B/572